THE OUTBACKERS

Books by Allan M Nixon

Bush Aussies
The Bushies (book & CD)
Beaut Utes 4
Beaut Utes 3
More Beaut Utes
Beaut Utes
Jokes for Blokes
Real Men Talking
Humping Bluey: Swagmen of Australia
Stand & Deliver: 100 Australian Bushrangers 1789–1901
Pocket Positives: A–Z of Inspirational Quotations
Somewhere in France: Sgt Roy Whitelaw AIF 1914–1918
The Swagmen: Survivors of the Great Depression
The Grinham Report: A Family History
100 Australian Bushrangers: 1789–1901
Inglewood Gold: 1859–1982
Inglewood: Gold Town of Early Victoria
Muddy Boots: Inglewood Football Club

Travelling the Outback with The Uteman

ALLAN M. NIXON

ABC
Books

Published by ABC Books for the
AUSTRALIAN BROADCASTING CORPORATION
GPO Box 9994 Sydney NSW 2001

Copyright © 2007 Allan M. Nixon

First published in March 2008

All rights reserved. No part of this publication
may be reproduced, stored in a retrieval system
or transmitted in any form or by any means,
electronic, mechanical, photocopying, recording
or otherwise, without the prior written permission
of the Australian Broadcasting Corporation.

ISBN 978 0 7333 2294 5

*Cover and internal design by Luke Causby / Blue Cork
Internals set in 12/18 pt Bembo by Kirby Jones*

DEDICATED TO PRO HART MBE
(1928–2006)

A true outbacker – an Aussie artist who
delighted millions around the world.
We shared many yarns and cuppas in studio,
shed, carport and at dining room table.
He influenced me greatly.
I shall never forget you,
and I miss ya, mate.

CONTENTS

MAP	VIII
STREWTH! ARE WE THERE YET?	1
THE LONG PADDOCK:	11
Col Hood, saddler	
TO MANFRED STATION:	53
Val, Peter and Tony 'Crowbar' Stead, the shearing Steads	
WHITE CLIFFS TO BOURKE:	81
Margaret Anne 'Ma' Baker, an outback opal	
FORDS BRIDGE TO TIBOOBURRA:	109
Andrea Rudd, Warrego Woman	
BROKEN HILL:	137
Howard William Steer, artback artist	
STILL IN BROKEN HILL:	151
Colin Warren, rabbit shooter and artist	
SILVERTON:	163
Andy Jenkins, coin cutter	
BROKEN HILL TO ARKAROOLA:	179
Bobby Shamroze, proud Afghan heritage	
MT HOPELESS:	199
Kye Crow and Gill Wheadon, cameleers	
LYNDHURST TO SOMEWHERE UNDER THE SOUTHERN CROSS	219
Talc Alf, talcum carver	
ARKABA:	243
Gordon Coulthard, one of the Rock People	
HAWKER TO THE FLINDERS RANGES:	255
Fred Teague, Mr Flinders Ranges	
THE GRAMPIANS TO BALLARAT:	269
Jon Muir and Seraphine Snupeson, a man and his dog	
DON'T LEAVE THE VEHICLE!	283
ACKNOWLEDGEMENTS	295

STREWTH!
ARE WE THERE YET?

I've sat through near 50°C heat and retreated underground to the coolness of opal mines at White Cliffs and Coober Pedy. I've sat on lonely hilltops and watched the eagles fly and the long, thin dust trails left by cattle as they move across the dry plains. I've flown in aircraft and helicopters to look at it all from high above. I've gone up and down rivers, watched the sun set across the salt lakes, and listened to rattling windmills turn in a night breeze. I've laid in many a swag and watched the brilliant night sky light up with falling stars. I've heard the dingoes howl and then dozed by a crackling fire of mulga. I've felt the early morning stiffness of white frost on a canvas swag by a desert creek.

That's the outback. And the people who live there I call the outbackers.

'Outbackers' is a term I came up with because I felt that we needed some Aussie lingo to recognise the people of the outback as distinct from those who are bushies. I've given the term a test run in the outback and people there love it and what it stands for – the tough men and women who fight the elements to survive, live and grow. Let's face it, it's easy to be called a bushie, but even people living in Bendigo and other regional cities are called that. The outbacker is a different person altogether.

So where is the outback exactly? You mention the outback to people who haven't been there and they think of Alice Springs, Ayers Rock and such. Hell, you don't have to go that far to meet great Aussie outbackers. The lifestyle Territorians live is not reserved just for them. Let me tell you, the sun gets just as hot in many places in the New South Wales and South Australian outback as it does in the Territory. The dust still blows and the rains flood. And anyway, there are too many tourists at Alice Springs and the like. I want you to see some different country, as well as meet some truly unforgettable people.

'A land of sweeping plains' – Allan Nixon a long way from home and still heading north.

If you're still in any doubt about where to find it, perhaps the following definition will help. When you are coughing on flies as you try to eat, you're being attacked ferociously by mosquitoes, the water in the billy boils without a fire, the sign says nearest petrol is 500 kilometres away, and as far as the eye can see there is 'nothing' – it's a fair chance you are within spittin' distance of the outback, or at least heading in the right direction.

The people in this book either live in the outback now or have lived there for many years before moving back to more settled lands. For the ones who moved away, the memories of days in the outback never leave them. I lived in Alice Springs in the 1970s and I can still clearly visualise what it was like then (much different to what it is now). In those days it was just a bush town, no traffic lights or malls or casinos or roundabouts. I loved to travel then and I've never stopped since; and the outback keeps calling me back – even more strongly in the last decade or so. There is something about it that never goes away once you've lived out there.

Outbackers know what it's like. They've seen it all before. The extreme heat, the dust and the flies. They've seen the rains and floods that come and go and take everything before them. They've seen the rise and fall of farming prices, and the despair that comes when stock and crops die in a drought. Dorothea Mackellar got it right when she described Australia as 'a sunburnt country, a land of sweeping plains', and talked about 'her beauty and her terror, a wide brown land …'

The people here have a story to tell of the place many fear and many love, of stony rock-hard deserts and sand that swallows your feet. This is their land, our land, yours and mine. This is spirit land. And you won't find any map that has a line showing the boundaries of the outback. Where is it? Trust me, you know when you get there. It is a special feeling. And these are the stories of the people who live there.

These are the outbackers.

Do you like to drive long distances?

No? Well, OK, you'd better sit back and let me do the driving. I love driving and spend months on the road, heading in all directions. This trip won't be that long for you, just a few thousand kilometres in a few weeks; not like the one I did with Mongrel, my mate. We crossed Australia twice in nineteen days doing 14,174 kilometres on as many rough dirt roads as we could find. We found them in five states and one territory (only missed going to Tassie and the ACT).

This is a trip out west, to western New South Wales, northwestern South Australia, and to the border of western Queensland. Out west is as much the outback as anywhere in the Territory if you stop, look and learn. This is 'the accessible outback', as one brochure calls the country near Broken Hill. But we still want to see more than just The Hill, so I've planned a sort of loop trip for you all. It isn't probably the trip you'd expect me to take you on, no out-of-the-way tourist attractions like Ayers Rock – and many of the places are just small country towns, nothing spectacular. But you'll see the red dust, the long, lonely tracks, the wild animals – and, of course, the characters who live there. This trip is to whet your appetite, to give you a glimpse of some of the people and places I've visited in the big sky country.

Who says where the outback is anyway? There are no lines on a map to say you've crossed the border into the outback country. Outback can be where you think it is – you will know it when you get there. It is a sense of being and a place in your mind.

I remember when I first drove from Mildura to Broken Hill, I really felt the further I went the more I was going into the outback. That's true, but now when I drive there, after having done it many, many times, it is like driving from Melbourne to Bendigo, Adelaide to Port Augusta, Sydney to Canberra, Brisbane to Byron Bay — there isn't a sense of the big adventure for me anymore. But I still love driving it. I love the feel of the road, the anticipation of seeing kangaroos and emus, the sunlight, the changing pattern of the landscape, and I never get sick of that first glimpse on the horizon of the ranges and mining poppet-head outlines of Broken Hill.

When I go outback, the place fills my mind and senses. I love travelling its roads and tracks.

Where did my love of travel come from? Family photo albums and diaries can pique a person's interest, and I suppose in my case that's what happened. One photo that comes to mind shows my

'Cutting a track as he went' – Grandfather changing a tyre during a hunting trip in 1920.

great-grandfather in a very early car next to a traction engine and loaded wool bales. However, one of the most evocative photos is of my grandfather changing a tyre on a 1920 Vinot car while his brother and others sit back and watch. The diaries of my grandfather also reveal his interest in driving and travel. His honeymoon in 1923 consisted of driving around the remote East Gippsland tracks to Mt Kosciuszko for a skiing holiday.

The old albums are full of his adventures in days when cars were still rare. He drove the first car to the top of Melville Caves, Victoria, cutting a track as he went. The local newspaper wrote up his adventures, and photos show him with a portable wireless on top of the car, listening to the Melbourne Cup. His detailed diaries and photographs always interested me and influenced me to go travelling too. He was a keen shooter, fisherman and outdoorsman. Much to my grandmother's disgust, she usually got the job of cleaning and cooking wild duck or fish. My grandmother told me many stories about grandfather's trips.

His photographs of those long-gone days still enthral me, and I can look at them for hours. I carry a small compass that was grandfather's all those years ago. It was given to me by my father.

Travelling has its drawbacks, of course. I'm often asked, whether I get lonely on my own in the outback. Aren't I afraid to go 'out there' on my own? Well, of course, it would be much better sometimes to have company on trips. But my work takes me to all sorts of places on my own, and companions won't always like travelling the distances I do, in the temperatures I sometimes travel in, on long, often exhausting trips. I can take half or even a whole day to interview, photograph and just yarn with people to do one story. When I leave, it may be late and I have to sleep wherever I can. That's OK if I'm towing a big caravan with all the mod cons, but more often than not I may just be in a ute, with only the swag and whatever food I think is needed for the trip. Now swagging it out underneath the stars can be romantic and enjoyable – it gets you back to the basics and I do enjoy that. But the desert nights, depending on the time of the year, can be freezing, and that's after days of over 40°C. Often I've woken up in a swag that's totally white with hard, crusty frost. I sleep well usually until early morning when the aches and pains of age start to rise in the body.

Not everyone likes to travel the outback like that, but if you come along with me you never know what the end of the day will bring. More often than not, I never know exactly where I'll end up.

Different seasons bring different conditions out here. We live in a land of extremes. As I write, it has been the worst drought on record, with bushfires in Victoria that burnt over a million square hectares in the high country. At the same time, there are floods making it tough in western Queensland; Birdsville and many other places are cut off from the rest of the world, and boats are the only way to get around.

Look at a big map of Australia. Follow the lines into the interior, away from the cities, and there's one thing you immediately see: there are a lot of roads that head outback. On a map, they might look like good roads linking one place to another. They do link places, but they aren't always good roads – in fact, many of them are rough and become impassable after rain.

So you still want to see the outback?

Good. Because although it may be harsh and sometimes dangerous, it is a magical place. Its beauty is grand, a country that fills every pore with wonder. It certainly isn't only Aboriginals who share the spirit of the land. Anyone who stands in the desert at Ayers Rock at sunset and can't feel the spirit of the land may as well stay in the suburbs, check off the Tattslotto numbers and settle in for a life of 'the boredom of normality'.

If you come to any part of the outback, be ready to absorb a new feeling.

Look beyond the heat, the flies, the dust and the 'nothingness'. Out here it all creeps up on you – new delights, sights, smells – and all the senses awaken. This is Australia. Take it in; you will never regret it. You will die happy – happy with memories of time spent in a land of contrasts, of beauty and harshness, simplicity and complexity, ruggedness and softness. The longer you spend out here the more the land fills your soul. When all else fails, just look up at a dark outback sky and find 'our' symbol: the stars of the Southern Cross.

A feeling is there for those who seek it – a place, a love, a warmth you can never fully describe. It's yours to keep, a gift from the great Australian outback. Come with me and let's see together what I've been seeing for years and desire for you to 'own' for yourself. I can't give it to you; I'm just your driver. I can introduce you to some of its people and its wonders, but I'll leave it up to you to take home what you want. I've been travelling it for over thirty years and there is still much more to see.

But the outback is more than the wide open spaces and the scenery; it is the people. I have sat over many a beer or cuppa yarning with outbackers. These are people who lead ordinary but interesting lives. This book is about some of my journeys and of the people I've met along the way, from a retired saddler and a shearing contractor to modern-day cameleers and successful artists.

If you take the time, you too can meet people like these and share some time with them. I urge you not to be like most tourists and just see the country from a car travelling at high speed. You'll miss the best part of the trip (and also high speed, in this unforgiving land, could kill you). Slow down, stop somewhere and experience what you find. Talk to people, relax and learn.

Well, the ute is packed and ready to go. This book will introduce you to some very different people, everyday Aussies who live they way they want to. You've never heard of most of them, but they are the people who make up the real Australia. If you want to meet real Aussies in real outback areas, then you are in for a treat.

'*A man with a thousand stories*' – saddlemaker Col Hood.

THE LONG PADDOCK

COL HOOD, SADDLER

'A tidy workshop is the devil's playground – that's why my workshop's a mess. I've never lost anything.'

The first person we will meet on out trip out west is Col Hood. The reason I'm putting him here is that his story will take in the country that you and I will be travelling through first. Col travelled the outback tracks in the 1950s in an old baker's cart towed by a horse; we'll be in an air-conditioned ute.

Col lives on a small property off the Hume Highway, but his life has included many kilometres outback, so I want to tell of his life. The area he traversed is now known as the Long Paddock – Col knows it well. This is the story of two young adventurers with stars in their eyes and of a youth who became a man – and a saddlemaker.

Within a few minutes of meeting Col Hood you know he is a man with a thousand stories. People like that have usually led a varied and interesting life. Col is such a bloke. Now retired at seventy-three, he still spends time in man's favourite domain – his shed. Nowadays, Col says he merely dabbles with leather, not like in the days when he created some of the most amazing western saddles – the type John Wayne, Gary Cooper and just about any other American cowboy used, whether on the big screen or in real life on the open range. 'I made about 200 western saddles when I lived in the USA for four years and many hundreds more over the years between when I made my first saddle in 1955 and when I gave it away in the late 1990s.'

Now he just repairs leather for friends on a casual basis. While the wood and leather rooms in his workshop don't hum like they might have once, they retain the look and sense that a real craftsman made his life here. There's some dust and cobwebs on the 150-plus-year-old sewing machine and everything has that 'worn but not wornout' look about it – it is great to spend time with a man who has made his interests his life's work. The red-roofed cottage on 10 acres was here before Ned Kelly was born, and through the lovely old peppercorn trees you can look across paddocks that join onto the Strathbogie Ranges.

Col was born in 1934 in Daylesford, Victoria, where his father was a hard-rock miner who supplemented his income with a gold mine in the backyard. 'When money was short the dynamite fuses got even shorter,' Col says with a grin. His family moved when he was three years old to East Preston in Melbourne. But more of Col's early life later.

First, I wanted more info, so as Col goes into his bunkhouse, Mary, his soulmate for the last thirteen years, sits down and I seek her views. Recovering from a back and hip operation, she is awaiting the arrival of the district nurse to change her dressings. Mary is from Shepparton and worked packing fruit in the orchard packing sheds for twenty-three years. Her son in Melbourne is about to make her a grandmother. Her daughter in Brisbane has four children already.

'Col has had a marvellous life really; his whole life is interesting – a very fulfilled life. He's a great man – a plumber, a builder – he can turn his hands to anything. A friend of his, Max McTaggart, a quarter-horse trainer, says Col is a genius, one-of-a-kind, and that he can do what others can't.'

As Col returns to the sunny dining room with a couple of boxes of photographs in hand, he says, 'Max is a very good horseman, one of the best. He lives for horses.' He adds with a laugh, 'He won't go to his own funeral unless there's also a horseshow.'

Mary and I return to our chat while Col starts to sort through the boxes. 'When my sister's husband died I went to help out on her horse agistment farm,' she says. 'I helped with the horses and loved them but wasn't a good rider. One day she sent me to Col to get him to fix a broken headstall for a horse, and then over a period I'd either drop off or pick up a piece of leatherwork of some sort and that's how we met, and things progressed from there. Col was divorced, had sadly lost a son in an accident. While I loved the racehorses my rheumatoid arthritis stopped all the plans for riding, but here with Col I do share in his love of horses. He sold his palomino mare "Missy" a couple of years ago – she was a pure-bred quarter horse.'

Col adds, 'Her real name was Miss Cutter Could – a real good-looking mare – she walked like Dolly Parton.' He points to some of the many photos on her new wall. 'That's her there, we stay in touch still with the owners. That's her with her new young foal.'

The walls of Col and Mary's cottage are covered in horse and western nostalgia. Many of the drawings and paintings of horses and scenes are Col's own handiwork. 'I'm a drawer not an artist,' he explains. The walls are also covered in memories: a framed and signed photo of Johnny Cash, an Indian war lance, and much cast-iron work such as blacksmith's tongs, stirrups, old kerosene lamps – almost anything country-, bush- or western-influenced. In one corner on a wooden stand specially built by Col is a beautifully hand-tooled western saddle made for Mary by Col. On a nearby shelf is a miniature of the same, equally as well crafted. The long table and chairs Col either made or restored. The chairs are leather carved by Col also. The entire rear part of the cottage was rebuilt by Col. This is a cosy home. I love its atmosphere and the yard and sheds and views across the brown land. I could live here.

'I don't even like going to town now,' says Mary. 'We are very happy here.'

Col is sorting through the boxes of photographs. The walls have large photos of Col on horseback in his early days. He is a lover of photography and I am interested to see more of his work, and particularly keen to see more of his trips by horse he's been telling me about. Finally I have to interrupt Col's many stories and take some notes, so it's time for me to ask the questions. I wonder how I am going to tell his life in a few pages. I know I can only scratch the surface and breeze over it, as his many yarns would fill a book. He says he's written his life story and writes articles for the *Australian Quarter Horse* magazine. He has already self-published a book called *Western Saddles: The Western Saddle Handbook*. He graciously signs a copy and presents it to me. He has also written poems and he illustrates everything with a clear, artistic hand.

So with a cuppa at hand I begin to ask Col my questions and know it will probably be hard to keep him on track – most old men have wonderful stories to tell. I warn him playfully I have to get his whole life into a few pages. He realises I will barely 'dip my pen in ink'. He will have to publish the full story.

'I'm studying structure and punctuation,' he says.

I reply, 'You're halfway there – you have your story out of your head and onto paper. That's more than what most people ever do.'

As I said, Col moved to East Preston with his family when he was three years old. Anyone who knows Melbourne suburbs will find it hard to believe it now, but in those days East Preston, from the end of Col's street out towards Greensborough, was mainly just open paddocks. Now it is busily suburban, with industrial estates, tramlines, and hustle and bustle.

'When I left school I got a five-year apprenticeship as an engineering patternmaker. Anything cast in metal would be first formed in wood, then from multiple moulds in sand, and you would pour molten metal to cast – we did all sorts of stuff like valves, water pipe fittings and any parts to do with machines. I finished my apprenticeship in 1954.

'At fifteen I had bought my first horse for £10. Then I thought, What the heck am I going to do with it now? I stole a piece of scaffolding rope to tether it. Anyway, it ended up in a paddock at the end of the street. Later I swapped it for a better one and that was how we grew to love them.

'My mates and I wanted to be like actor Chips Rafferty. I bought a stockwhip and from then on, nothing was safe – I'd crack it, the cat and the chooks would scatter, none of Mum's flowers were safe. I cracked it until the end was off it. "There's a man in Thornbury who will fix it for you," I was told – and that was how I met my mentor and teacher, John G. Chirnside. What a man. He went to the USA to live in 1959, bud sadly he died of cancer in 1973. He was a fine guitar player and horseman, and a thorough gentleman.

'Anyway, I went to his backyard workshop – an Aladdin's cave of leatherwork – horse gear, waist-belts ... and a western saddle. That's what got me going. I spent hours talking with him and looking.

'"Will you fix my stockwhip?" I asked.

'"No," he replies offhandedly. I was shocked and disappointed.

'"You can fix it, but I will teach you."

'He also taught me how to braid leather. I was hooked. His workshop was only a mile or so from my home, so I ended up going there a lot. I admired the western saddle – one day he let me put it on my horse and go for a ride. It was so comfortable and I said, "Why don't you make more?"

'"I can't get a saddle tree," he said, and so I said I could make him one as I was a woodworker. He said OK, but why don't I make two saddle trees and we'll make two saddles and he'll teach me. So we did, but halfway through making the saddles I told him I was heading north with a mate.

'Neville Page was a good mate of mine. We knocked around on horses together and we both wanted to be Chips Rafferty and ride across the land droving cattle, just like him as the stockman in the movie *The Overlanders*. One day Nev said, "Why don't we go bush?" So I say, "OK" – and that was it. He drove a baker's cart for a job, so said he'd start to look for one for us to use on the trip. Later he said he'd found an old one in Clifton Hill for £5,

'The things young adventurers will do' – Neville Page at the reins.

so we draped harness gear over my horse, both jumped on and rode to Clifton Hill, paid for it, harnessed the horse to it, and drove home. It was like an old hawker's van, but someone had changed the wooden spoke wheels for A-model Ford car wheels, pressed steel and rubber tyres. Later we saw an old abandoned A-model car in the yard of a sheep station where we worked. It had better tyres, so we pinched them and swapped them over for ours.'

That cheeky grin appears on Col's face again. The things young adventurers will do. Nowadays, they'd pinch the whole car as well.

'Originally six of us mates were going to go, but the other four pulled out. Years later they said they'd wished they'd gone with us too. Anyway, Nev and I took off from East Preston and then went to South Morang, Mernda, Whittlesea (camped by the cemetery), across to Sydney Road at Wallan, on through Kilmore, Broadford, Elmore, Rutherglen, Echuca, up the Cobb Highway to Pretty Pine, Deniliquin, Wanganella, Hay, One Tree, Booligal, Ivanhoe,

Wilcannia, up the Paroo River to Copargo Station (part of Kidman's Mombo Station). We did general station work where we could get it along the way, but sometimes nothing was available. We went up the Paroo to Wanaaring, then to Hungerford on the Queensland border. We still picked up a day's work here and there; on to Thargomindah, Eromanga to Cooper Creek (few jobs). We got a droving job to go to Quilpie. We went out west where the drovers go and I saw a great deal of the country. I had to head back to Melbourne to be best man at my sister's wedding, but I returned again to go droving. We'd left our horses on the common at Windorah, but when I returned they were gone, nowhere to be found. The old baker's cart we'd left behind the pub. Neville had gone off on his own and eventually joined Lofty Kennard's Travelling Buckjump Show, or whatever it was called.

'I'd spent a while along the Cooper as a drover and stockman, then I got to thinking, I really don't want to end up as an old drover, drinking too much and boasting in the pub. So that was where my droving days ended. For eighteen months we'd wandered about doing it – it taught me "keep your horses alive and you'll stay alive – and let nothing daunt you". By now we had a team of four horses in the wagon. It was 1956, the year of the big floods, and I arrived home just in time for Christmas and then went straight to Walhalla to pan for gold, but no go. In early 1957 I bought a motorbike and finished making my first saddle with my friend Chirnie. I took a job as a patternmaker at Gatic foundry, but soon went out to be a self-employed saddlemaker.'

Col married, but it is here we move forward some years as it is obvious some painful memories exist, especially to do with losing a son.

'In 1971 a friend said to come to Buffalo River in northeast Victoria – there's a house on 1000 acres right on the lake, you can have for as long as you want. To be on such a magnificent property was just magic. Years later after I'd left, I went back to find they'd destroyed it all and planted pine trees.

'In 1976 I bought this cottage on 10 acres. A sad break in my life occurred in 1984, though, and I lived and worked for a short time in a packing shed and loft at Wandon, Victoria.

'Between 1986 and 1990 I lived in the USA, where I worked as a saddlemaker. Not exactly legal, so I had to lose the Australian ocker accent and fit right in as a cowboy. I lived in Nebraska, but did travel everywhere west of the Mississippi, from Mexico right up to Alaska. I did a lot of saddlework and general leatherwork. I even ended up with my own business called C.H. Saddlery, Custom Makers, Minatare, Nebraska. I travelled to rodeos and things like the

'The number one western saddlemaker' – Col with one of his creations.

Frontier Days at Cheyenne, Wyoming, or to Denver, but I was really just dancing, partying, shooting pool, drinking Budweiser and being somebody. That was great. I'd worked in the Nebraska Panhandle making saddles, worked behind the bar, doing anything – house maintenance, sign writing and playing cowboy.'

Col's life has been much more than being a travelling cowboy. Saddlemaking, particularly making western saddles, has been a big part of his life, and many people who now own a Col Hood western saddle are lucky to have them. While he doesn't promote it, I saw photos and clippings of his career as 'the number one western saddlemaker'. Indonesian President Suharto and his son invited Col overseas, where he made saddles for both of them. Others who can say they have sat in a Col Hood saddle include US actor Hugh O'Brien, who played Wyatt Earp in the TV series, as well as Lorne Greene, famous as Ben Cartwright on the *Bonanza* TV series. ('I don't believe he was a great rider,' Col says of Greene.)

I asked Col what else he made apart from western saddles.

'All sorts of stuff – bridling, gun holsters, handbags and waistbelts by the millions.' It used to take him weeks to make a saddle, but he is reluctant to say exactly how much he charged. Just by their quality you know they aren't cheap. Handmade, beautifully crafted and carved, you know they are the best. 'An old horseman once said to me that saddle prices are always around the same price as the horse: £25 for the saddle, £25 for the horse. In 1955 I got £35 for a saddle, in the '80s I got US$1500.'

There are a lot of good saddlemakers in Australia now. And good craftsmen deserve to be paid well. So what does a craftsman do when he thinks it's time to give up full-time work and retire? Go play in his shed, of course.

'A self-employed saddlemaker' – a younger Col Hood at his trade.

Nowadays, Col spends a lot of time on the computer. 'I'm more interested in getting all my stories written down. I write poems also, do some drawings and enjoy life. My life – apart from being great – is becoming an elder-statesman of my craft when young people want to know your opinion, and that helps keep you confidence up. I've passed on saddlemaking to about half-a-dozen young people really interested in it. Now I'm the mentor, just like J.G. Chirnside was to me all those years ago. I'm highly respected – they're not my words, other people's words who respect my work.'

I want to take some of Col's leatherwork home with me, so he and I spend time, after lunch with Mary, in the shed. I watch as Col hammers out a small piece of carved leather for me, showing and explaining what each of his tools is for. 'My eyes aren't as good now. I can't see,' he says, as he adjusts the light and reaches for another pair of glasses.

Shortly after, he's finished. And as we shake hands I leave with a good feeling, knowing I have spent time with Col Hood – master craftsman.

Back on the road again and we are heading towards the roads that Col Hood got to know well. For this trip we shall start at Echuca and have a quick rest there to enjoy the sights and sounds of the mighty Murray River. For me, the river is therapy, it is always soothing and a great way to start a trip outback. Often I stay right opposite the historic wharf, in room 8 on the first floor of the historic Steampacket Inn. Why? Because it overlooks the Murray right on the bend where all the paddleboats pull in, steam whistles blowing – a great feeling for a writer. Other times, when I want to relax elsewhere, there are numerous caravan parks right on the water's edge. Sometimes I've been lucky enough to actually be allowed to sleep on board the paddleboat, the *Henry Charles*, but that is another story.

This is a book about travelling in outback areas away from rivers usually, so we shall be gone in the morning. Sleep. We will be up early. Six am on the river is a magic time of day.

A WORD ON SIGNS

We cross the bridge at Echuca and go past Moama, and head for the Cobb Highway, which we'll follow along the full length of the Long Paddock – over 600 kilometres. We are following the same route that Col Hood did all those years ago. From here on we will be reading a lot of signs and be on the lookout for them. Signs are very much part of daily life – we are so inundated with signs that we miss most of them; we ignore them or try to ignore them, or we have got used to having so many in our lives that we simply switch off.

I bet if the next time you are driving and you ask your companions in the vehicle what the previous sign said, or how many kilometres to the next stop, or any number of questions related to what a sign might say, most will simple not know. That's because we only read them when we have to, usually only if we are not sure of where we are going. But signs can make a boring trip interesting. You can often learn something of the local history or what the locality is. For instance, if you saw a sign that said 'Paddleboat Lagoon', what would you expect to find there? Often I have found stories by simply doing a U-turn and going to look at unusual signs. Sometimes it is a waste of time, other times great fun. I've taken some great photos by simply following my instincts and taking a detour. Sadly, most people nowadays (and sometimes me included) are often too busy to take the time to explore. Signs can also be a bloody pain.

I always read unusual signs, not the ones like Stop, Go, Give Way or U-turn and all those – ignore them (joke, Joyce!). I mean the ones on the road that say 5 kilometres to Wonganamunullabibybob Creek or Kimmyinyecricket Tank or the ones like 'Wallawallanullanulla – Gateway to the Riverina'. Ever notice how many 'gateways' there are? They are always saying that such-and-such a place is a gateway to somewhere else. It is like someone is saying, 'Well, you're here, but it isn't much good, so keep going and you'll get there.' Other types of signs amuse me. 'Australia's wheat belt town', or 'Australia's best wheat town'. How many wheat towns are there in Australia? I've seen quite a few.

Then, of course, we have the 'heart of' towns – Heart of the Murray, Heart of the Outback, Heart of the Blowflies and Dunny

Town. Fair dinkum. I can't wait to read a town sign that gives the truth: 'Ooliedoolie – Prick of a Town and Nothing to See or Do, Tourists Piss Off'.

The ones that really cheese me off are the signs out in the middle of bloody nowhere, usually near a paddock of scungy crop withering into the dust, miles from absolutely everywhere, and a huge sign says something like 'Welcome to the Great City of Bendigo'. Or there's one on the Hume Highway heading north that says: 'Welcome to the Macedon Ranges Wine District'. The bloody ranges are frigging miles away to the southwest, and where this sign is located, the only thing that resembles a mountain is the leftover load of road screenings that the Highways Department dumped there ten years ago and forgot to clean up! The nearest thing to wine around here is an empty bottle of McWilliams Sherry that someone threw into the grass. This is the Hume Highway; the Macedon Ranges is on the Calder Highway.

But what can make an interesting trip turn into a boring one are the main stops pointing out supposed historical places of interest. Take, for example, 'Site of the Upper Kumbutcha Primary School 1896'. All that is left is an empty paddock surrounded by a broken-down fence, and a blown-over tank and stand riddled with bullet holes, plus weeds by the ton. If you're lucky, you might see a peppercorn tree and some broken bricks. The sign doesn't tell you when it was there, what happened to it, if there is a mass grave or the ghost of a teacher hanged by vigilante adolescents, or anything else that might intrigue the mind. It says once there was something here – now there isn't.

The ones I really enjoy are the 'trails' – those former routes taken by settlers, Cobb & Co coaches, cattlemen, drovers and such. Nowadays, many shires are getting largish grants to install signs along routes to highlight features on what can often be a boring drive. Signs or memorials that annoy me are the ones when you stop to read a 'historic memorial' and find it is just a brag site for local toffs. This sort of thing:

'Cr Tommy T. Ticker, JP, MP, AOM, VC, AO, CBE and Mayor of Snake Creek, opened this memorial to Tommy T. Ticker and his family who have held sway over 2 million acres in this country since 1856. This rubbish bin memorial was unveiled in the presence of J. Howard Prime Minister, M. Turnbull Minister for the Environment, and an entourage of 43 bureaucrat hangers-on; Cr J.J. Ticker, Cr S.T. Ticker, Cr H.G. Ticker, and Jack Dooley local Member for Ticker Shire. After an afternoon of music by the local brass band, the ribbon was duly cut by Mrs Yvonne Ticker, wife of T.T. Ticker, ably assisted by His Right Honorable T.T. Ticker. Afternoon tea of cakes and sandwiches was duly supplied to the CWA Ladies' Tennis Guild, ably supported by IGA Grocers, Tom's BP Service Station and Sully's Royal Mail Pub. This memorial cost $1 million and was paid for by 17 Federal, State and Local Government Department Grants [i.e. taxpayers].'

Some memorials make great deeds out of local history: 'Jack Dowling's dog Missy took a piss on this now dead tree in 1943.'

Good excuse to put up a rubbish bin that never gets emptied, a toilet block that stinks like all hell and would make you pray for constipation, and a water tap that either doesn't work or vandals have smashed it and water has been leaking out of for twenty-three months and there's still no sign of a maintenance crew.

So from here on we are looking for a lot of signs and we will stop and take photographs along the way.

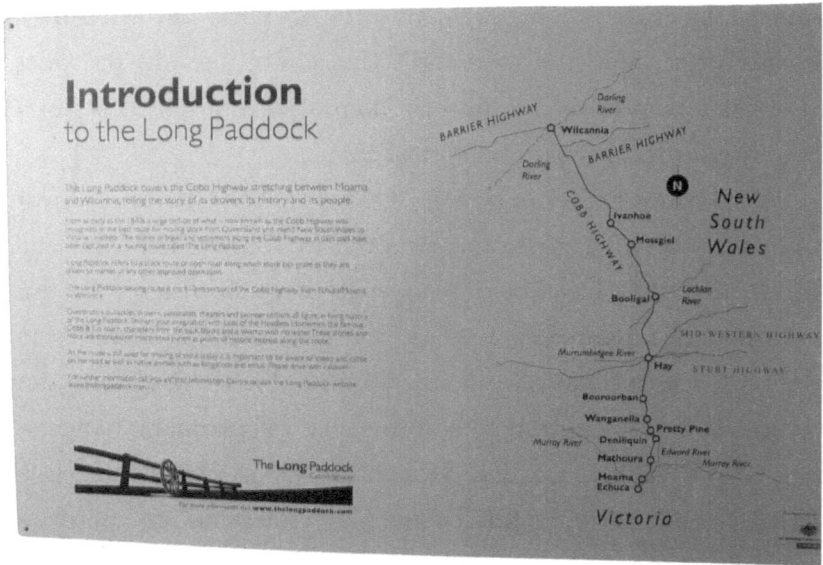

'Good history lessons' – Long Paddock tourist sites of the Cobb Highway.

THE LONG PADDOCK SITES

The route we now travel is a historic highway indeed. Since the 1840s it has been an important stock route, and you will learn something about our pioneers, drivers, bullockies, Aborigines, truck drivers, settlers and more.

The brochures all proudly talk of the huge, wide-open plains. The one thing they don't promote very well when discussing the Long Paddock sites along the travelling stock route (TSR) of the Cobb Highway, from Echuca–Moama to Wilcannia, is the fact that you pass across or near some of Australia's better known rivers – Murray, Murrumbidgee, Lachlan, Darling and Edward. In 2007 it is a time of drought, but nevertheless the rivers remain, just not in their best dress.

The *Macquarie Dictionary* explains that the term 'long paddock' is 'a stock route or open road, especially regarded as a place where people, too poor to own their own paddocks or pay for agistment, can graze their horses, cattle etc'. Long paddocks are also used by landowners when feed in their own area is scarce due to drought. This has been a way of life in many parts of Australia since settlement began. Today there are traditional stock routes still in use, but many are now facing closure for a variety of reasons.

The Long Paddock tourist sites of the Cobb Highway are a good example of what can be done to liven up a boring drive. From Echuca–Moama, the Cobb passes through Deniliquin, Hay, Booligal, Mossgiel and Ivanhoe before ending at Wilcannia, through the long, long flat plains made famous by Henry Lawson's and Banjo Paterson's poems. The highway takes people across what some say is the largest plain in the world. What they leave out is that this is also one of the most boring drives as well. Look at any comments on the internet, and the Long Paddock will invariably be described as 'bored shitless' country or 'godforsaken hell hole' country, and many other similar comments. The new signs make stops worthwhile – they are good history lessons, even if 10,000 blowflies stick to you as soon as you open your vehicle door. (I love to take off, get up speed and then hit the electric windows down and blow the little blighters out at 100 km/h. Of course, there are those wise to your pathetic attempt at mass destruction, and cling to anything within sight.)

There is no doubt it can be a boring drive – if you want it to be – or you can set your mind to thinking about the old days of drovers and their stock, and get a feel for how tough it was. A bit hard, maybe, seeing as we have the air-conditioner on and our choice of music blaring. Nowadays, too, kids spend their time in the back seats glued to those electronic game thing-y-mabobs. If you stop to read the signs on the roadside, don't be surprised if the kids pretend they are asleep in order to avoid getting out. Kids aren't as curious these days as they once were.

White-man exploration of this vast area commenced in 1817 with the explorer John Oxley, who, over the next twenty years, was followed by Charles Sturt and Thomas Mitchell. River and grasslands then attracted squatters and settlers, and soon towns developed near the rivers. In the 1850s Victorian goldfields needed to be fed, which led to the development of this stock route. Settlers also moved stock north or south in drought times to as far as Queensland in search of feed. The river systems also meant that riverboats carried wool, supplies and people. Cobb & Co coaches developed a vast network of routes, which resulted in more and more people coming to the regions.

As we travel north, the driver is constantly in the sun until the afternoon, when the passenger gets the heat of the day. We will be travelling north to the Darling.

YELLOW WATERHOLES

Our first stop is just 18 kilometres north of Moama at Yellow Waterholes. Nothing much to see, but in 1867 this was a stock watering point, and for eight years the Duke of Edinburgh Inn was open for business. Approximately 2 kilometres to the south of where I am standing now, a clump of trees is believed to be all that remains of the inn site. History recalls that Yellow Waterholes was a spot to negotiate bad track and also to pay for the right to pass through a paddock – the cost was often one sheep. The largest landholder, Sir John O'Shannassy, the owner of Moira Station, was the centre of controversy, with small selectors and drovers wishing to drive through his property. In 1875 one incident saw horsemen from O'Shannassy's place demanding five shillings per team from several bullock teams and drovers. The teams refused to pay and eventually summonses were issued. O'Shannassy was a parliamentarian who knew how to throw his weight around.

A few more kilometres on and we see Moira Station on the right, but it was not the first station – the original was built in the 1840s. The Moira Inn stood nearby, and eventually in 1862 it was Sir John O'Shannassy who bought the 100,000-plus-acre property. He built the present home and a 32-stand woolshed. Sir John was Victorian premier three times. He vehemently opposed selectors' attempts to take up land near his property, and one long and bitter case he carried on with a William Joachim was finally settled by the Privy Council in London. Joachim won, but lost almost everything except the land he had selected in his children's names.

MATHOURA

It was timber-getters, saw millers and charcoal burners who helped Mathoura, about 40 kilometres north of Moama, prosper and grow. Timber from the river red gum forests supplied fencing, wharf piles, railway sleepers and wood for paddleboats. Even the streets of Melbourne were once paved with blocks from the local forests.

In 1865 Henry Burton bought the Redbank Inn. He was known as Australia's Father of the Circus because he had formed the first touring circus in 1850. A special ring was built and his animals were trained at Redbank in winter. He became Mathoura's first postmaster.

'Towed by twelve horses' – a log wagon built in 1926 at Mathoura.

Outside the tourist information office is a log wagon built in 1926 by Jim Buchanan. It was towed by twelve horses to carry logs from Gulpa Island forest and could carry up to 3500 super feet (13 tonnes) of heavy red gum.

DENILIQUIN

About 35 kilometres further on, time for lunch in Deniliquin and some refuelling of the ute. I sit in the ute near the Edward River, which passes through town, and in the shade of some lovely peppercorns trees. A delightful rest stop right in town. Not far away I can see a Holden ute atop a huge steel pole – Deniliquin is the self-proclaimed ute capital of the world.

Deniliquin is situated 700 kilometres from Sydney. The area around it produces rice, wool, dairy products, wheat, barley, fat lambs, vegetables and fruit, timber and cattle. Local industry includes rice and timber mills.

The first inn went up in about 1845 and the town site was finally gazetted in 1850, the year a store and post office opened. It became an important river crossing for stock as it was situated at the end of three major stock routes from Queensland and New South Wales to Victoria. Settlement continued on both sides of the river. The two parts of the town were finally joined when the first bridge was opened in 1861.

Deniliquin tourist brochures describe the town as 'an oasis of green on the edge of the Riverine plain, which stretches northwards in what is the flattest land on earth – welcome to the beginning of the outback. Deniliquin is situated on the Edward River, in the centre of Riverina sheep station country and on the fringe of the world's largest red-gum forest …'

Well, as for 'the flattest land on earth', we don't think so. In fact the Hay Plains to the north are only the second largest and flattest in Australia and certainly not the world; and the 'largest red-gum forest' is a fair bit south, closer to Mathoura than here. Sounds good in a brochure, though.

I don't see Deniliquin as an oasis. It is a largish country town that serves a good farming community, but it is isolated more than some and closer to civilisation than others. It has good sporting facilities. It is a typical bush town. It is home to Australia's largest ute show, which I attend each year along with thousands of others and a pack of exuberant police from the city and bush who see it as a great weekend to make a heap of money for the New South Wales Treasury, fines of every description being handed out to anyone game enough to look sideways. Without them, though, the event would be a total free-for-all. The ute show weekend is

'One of Australia's greatest inventions' – a crazy ute at the Deniliquin Ute Muster.

an extremely popular event that has been going on for nearly ten years. Some of Australia's greatest musical talent (and not so great) put on non-stop music in the dust or mud each year. About 6000 utes park in an open paddock, and people enjoy a weekend of fun, booze and fun, with great utes on display and bombs out the back as well. Nowhere is there an event where as many utes get together. To ute lovers, it is what part of heaven may look like.

The ute is one of Australia's greatest inventions, recognised the world over. The first manufactured one-piece-bodied ute was designed by Australian Lew Bandt at Ford Geelong in 1932. This model went into successful production and sales in 1934 and is now a treasured collector's item. Henry Ford in America described it as 'an Aussie Kangaroo chaser'. Ford is the longest continual manufacturer of utes in Australia.

Deniliquin has some nice attractions in and around town – gardens, old buildings – and visitors should check it all out at the

Peppin Heritage Centre near the bridge over the Edward. The centre contains the original Wanganella lockup, which features the Headless Horseman sound and light show. (More of him later up the track at Black Swamp.)

Not many people would realise that bushrangers came here. Island Sanctuary, in the river, is supposed to be the final resting place of Old Jack, a member of the Melville gang, bushrangers who visited Deniliquin in 1851. According to local information, Old Jack was so drunk that his companions tied him to a tree and threw turpentine over him, thinking it was water. As his hollering increased, one gang member approached him with a candle and Jack burst into flames. Once untied, he threw himself in the river but died after two days.

Time to hit the road.

PRETTY PINE

Just 32 kilometres from Deniliquin, I stop outside the Pretty Pine Hotel.

Pretty Pine was originally called The Junction because of its location at the point where the Cobb Highway meets Moulamein Road. In the early days, a travelling judge, Judge Francis, would stop off under a handsome pine tree, and in 1865 he got authorities to change the locality's name to The Pretty Pine. When an inn was built, it became known as the Pretty Pine once its licence was issued. Cobb & Co coaches stopped here. The area was called the 12 Mile Stables. A hawker, George Myzan, was murdered not far from here, and amid much controversy, Joseph Cordone was hanged in Deniliquin Gaol in 1884 for the murder.

There's still a hotel here, but it's not the original, which burnt down in 1916. The pine tree outside the Pretty Pine Hotel has had

'A handsome pine tree' – Pretty Pine Hotel today.

the gong. It's kaput, cactus, knackered, stuffed. Dead as a maggot. It stands out like a cat at dog school. Other trees give nice shade and the lawn is still pretty green considering the drought. It looks like a nice little pub and I know it is popular. But when I arrived it was closed. I will return to find out more about the tree. Was it the one Judge Francis so admired? It doesn't look old enough. Did I miss seeing the real pretty pine? I shall return to find out one day.

PEPPIN RAM MEMORIAL

Did you know that one in every 200 sheep is allergic to wool?

Just south of Wanganella is the Peppin Memorial, a large statue of a sheep on a block of granite, which stands on a cement base that's in the shape of Australia. Apart from the ever-present flies and the crows scavenging through an overflowing rubbish bin, I was the sole visitor this day.

In 1858 George Peppin & Sons bought Wanganella Station and in 1861 founded a merino stud. Their stud included the famous ram Emperor and, by 1878 when they sold out, they had created a foundation stock for many famous studs of Peppin blood strain in Australia. About 85 per cent of Australia's merino sheep have the Peppin strain in their bloodlines.

One of the plaques on the statue gives some interesting statistics for Australian sheep production over 100 years.

	1861	1961
Sheep Production	20,000	153,000,000
Wool Production	67,000,000 lb	1,627,000,000 lb
Wool cut per head	3.35 lb	10.63 lb
Merino Wool Prices	22d per lb	70d per lb
Value of Wool Clip	£6,000,000 approx	£314,500,000

Foundation stock – Peppin Ram Memorial, just south of Wanganella.

WANGANELLA

About 8 kilometres on, Wanganella is a nice spot surrounded by trees, with a shop and a shelter devoted to the history of Cobb & Co. It's a great place to yarn to the nice lady in the shop and have a yarn with her dog. I wonder if passengers on Cobb & Co coaches would have agreed with this description of coach travel out here placed as an advertisement in a Deniliquin newspaper in the 1860s: 'There is something bracing, clear and exhilarating in coach travelling and it would be hard to beat the style of tonic one gets on a summer morn, seated behind a spanking team which bowls over roads and bush tracks beneath fragrant trees.'

Well, not out here, mate. More likely, the passengers would have been rocked and rolled, thrown about on either dirty or muddy tracks, bogged, and subjected to flies, heat, cold and rain in a long, boring landscape where seeing a tree would have brought relief, before arriving at their destination, jaded and exhausted.

It is in Wanganella country, famous for the Peppin Stud, that we can see some of the reason why the stud prospered. The

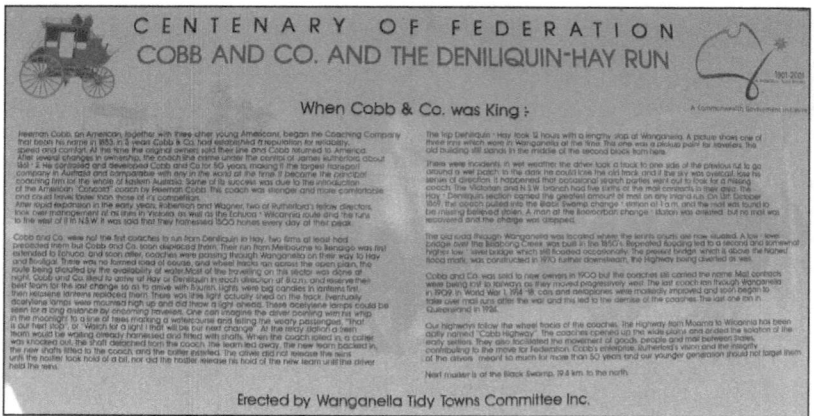

'When Cobb & Co was king' – Wanganella, a great spot to take in some local history.

country from here on northwards becomes what is known as the Saltbush Plains – and Banjo Paterson describes it: 'To those that love it and understand, the Saltbush Plains are a wonderland. A wondrous land where nature's ways were revealed to me in the Droving Days.'

Saltbush continues to grow throughout long periods of drought, and while settlers weren't too impressed with it at first, they soon learnt the value of the Riverina saltbush and other native herbage vegetation, which are the mainstays of the grazing industry. There are many species, including oldman saltbush, the smaller, abundant bladder saltbush – both of which have a high salt content – and a range of smaller saltbushes, bluebushes, cotton bush and other related species.

BLACK SWAMP

Drovers around Black Swamp in the middle of the nineteenth century told of a horseman who appeared suddenly at a camp site, mounted on a trotting horse, a cloak about his shoulders but with no head, spooking animals and causing stampedes. Some claim it to have been the ghost of a drover who died at the swamp. One story has it that a Moulamein butcher took advantage of the tale: dressing himself in a cloak thrown over a wooden frame on his shoulders, which gave him the appearance of being headless, he is said to have pinched small numbers of cattle for his own profit.

There are numerous versions of the story, featuring stampedes, major thefts and droving of stolen cattle across the border for sale in Victoria. One version says the horseman was shot and killed; another claims that he was never captured. A Cobb & Co driver claimed he carried the wounded thief to a hospital, where he died, but the driver later saw the headless body of the same man on his horse.

It thus seems unclear whether the thief took advantage of an existing myth or whether the myth arose from his activities. We shall never really know the truth. Whatever the substance of the legend, there is no doubt that it exists, and at the Black Swamp travellers can retell the story and send chills down the kids' spines as they tell them of the headless horseman riding on a dark and filthy night on the open plains of yesteryear.

Woooooooo!

BOOROORBAN

I drive on for 30-odd kilometres to Booroorban, in the middle of the Old Man Plain. The Booroorban Hotel features the Headless Horseman Bar.

'The Royal Mail Hotel' – former drover Frances relaxes outside the pub.

Beneath some well-established peppercorn trees stands the Royal Mail Hotel, which was built by Samuel Porter in 1868. Booroorban owes its origins to the hotel, which was a staging post on the Cobb & Co run between Hay and Deniliquin. Passengers disembarked while the horses were exchanged for a fresh team kept in the stables at the rear of the hotel. Bullock teams carried wool to Echuca and Bendigo and returned with goods for the locals. At one time the area was known as Pine Ridge. By 1885 there were two hotels, a school, post office, general store, some other public buildings and about 200 residents. Little remains, but the Royal Mail is a nice spot for a stop and to enjoy more peppercorn trees.

It annoys me that today many councils across the country destroy peppercorns because they are 'not native to Australia', as one councillor said to me. I pointed out they were destroying our pioneering heritage, as you can be sure that if you see peppercorn trees there is or was some early building nearby. Settlers always planted peppercorns. Some country towns have beautiful streets lined with peppercorns. This country has many trees that originated overseas. The street where I live has over a kilometre on both sides of the road of beautiful 150-year-old English oak trees. I can imagine the uproar if the council tried to remove them. Councils are selective with their 'not native' approach to tree removal.

I've heard claims that the trees have white-ants, that flies and mosquitoes breed in them, and other claims as well. I've never seen a white-ant-infested dying or dead peppercorn. I don't recall being eaten by mozzies while sitting under a peppercorn tree – ever.

I remember years ago I planted a peppercorn on the nature strip outside my home when I lived in Melbourne. My mother was horrified, saying, 'You can't plant those in Melbourne, they only belong in the bush.' When I sold the house many years later, the new owner cut out every tree on the nature strip – except the peppercorn, which is now as tall as the house and adds a beauty to the street that many people admire.

16 MILE GUMS

Around 25 kilometres later, a stop out in the middle of nowhere is made easier by sitting in the shade of a nice, flourishing eucalyptus. Here at the 16 Mile Gums, however, there are signs of great stress. The thin line of trees very much look like they are dying. The drought has hit hard. Years ago this was a welcome stopover for travellers.

A sign tells me about the place: 'In 1863 W.H. Beresford established the Settlers Arms here which met all the requirements of passing coaches and drovers of sheep and cattle. It was the last of five change stations between Deniliquin and Hay. This was no small place, the Settlers had a total of twelve rooms, a kitchen and other outbuildings, stables and stockyards, complete with stock troughs. The Settlers closed with the expiration of the final licence owned by Edward Brandon in 1879. Some years later the Government Tank which was a short distance away was used as a mail coach change. Surrounding this area in later years were a large number of selections and settlement leases. The 16 Mile Gums Hotel continued to serve many patrons for many years.'

To get an idea of just how important stopovers were in the 'good old days' we only have to look at some of the facts. As late as the 1950s more than 30 million sheep – a quarter of the total Australian flock – as well as between 4 and 5 million cattle, passed

'The drought has hit hard' – 16 Mile Gums.

'Signs of great stress' – 16 Mile Gums.

'On the wide open plains' – 16 Mile Gums in the distance on a long flat road.

along stock routes each year. These routes were administered by the Pastoral Protection Board, and sheep had to be moved 6 miles each day. The sheep were not allowed to travel the same ground twice unless ownership of the stock had changed hands. Cattle had to move 10 miles a day. In the 1950s, owners were charged about £25 per 100 head of sheep each week to travel the Long Paddock.

Some more information on the sign tells me that 'At the 16 Mile Gums, some seventy cattle could be watered at a time, the rest of the herd would be held back and it would take three to four hours to water most herds. Between Hay and the 16 Mile bore there are three other bores – the 7 Miles, 10 Miles and the 12 Miles bores.'

What a pity if all these trees were left to die on the wide open plains. Let's hope local shires can do something to save them. However, with the drought affecting many people in many ways, I think the 16 Mile Gums may be last on the list for assistance, which is a pity, as a long-term look at tourism should be taken into account. If they want people to continue to drive the Long Paddock, shires need to keep the few attractions alive. The trees at the 16 Mile Gums deserve it. It would also be a good spot to enhance as a stopover spot for campers and caravaners. But it certainly needs some work – now.

I should point out that there has been some considerable work done at the 16 Mile Gums: Greening Australia, Natural Heritage Trust and Hay Pastoral Protection Board have all had involvement here, according to signs. Water pipes and fenced-off areas no doubt help. Unfortunately, not all the trees are fenced off and most seem to be just hanging on. If the trees returned to their former glory, this would be a great place to stop.

HAY

I don't need to remind you that a great deal of Australia is flat, with only the eastern part of the continent lacking extensive plains. The Hay Shire is located on the vast open and virtually treeless plain first commented upon by the early explorers and known today as the Hay Plains of New South Wales. The plains are recognised as one of the flattest sections of land in the world, the second-flattest in Australia – there is only 17 metres difference between the highest and lowest points. The Murrumbidgee and Lachlan rivers are the major systems. Reduced water flows, in particular in the Lachlan, have meant that the river red gum forests are slowly reducing in size. The Hay Plains were predominantly sheep country in the old days, as they are now. These days, Hay is promoted as the home of Shear Outback, the Australian Shearers' Hall of Fame.

I like Hay. It is an attractive town that has preserved its peppercorns!

It is an important pastoral centre, on the Murrumbidgee River at the junction of the Sturt, Cobb and Mid Western highways,

'The home of Shear Outback' – the Australian Shearers' Hall of Fame, Hay.

halfway between Sydney and Adelaide. Flat, open, treeless saltbush plains surround the town.

Charles Sturt explored the Murray and Murrumbidgee rivers in 1829–30, passing by the future town site in his whaleboat. There is a monument in Sturt Park (on Lachlan Street) to commemorate his journey.

River-steamer captain Francis Cadell built a store at the river crossing here in 1858. Murrumbidgee Punt Hotel and the establishment of the township were gazetted in 1859.

Cobb & Co made Hay the headquarters of their Victoria and Riverina operations from 1862 to 1896. A brass band greeted the arrival of the company's coaches, feed wagons, twenty drivers, 103 horses, plus cooks and ostlers. The company set up a coach factory at the corner of Lachlan and Simpson streets in 1877.

Joseph Furphy, who lived in Hay while bullock carting about the region in the 1870s, set much of his famous novel *Such is Life* (1903) within the district. In World War II Hay was used as a POW and internment centre.

In the main street, on the corner near the information centre, you can peer into a shop window and see 'Sunbeam', a Cobb & Co coach. Built locally in 1886, it ran on the Deniliquin to Wilcannia line. It was used in the 1975 film *Mad Dog Morgan*.

Hay Gaol has seen a few changes in its time. It was built in 1879 to replace an earlier prison, and closed in 1915, only to reopen six years later as a maternity hospital. It became a prison again in 1930, and in World War II was used to house prisoners of war. The last POWs left in 1947. From 1961 to 1974 it housed 'incorrigible girls' brought from Sydney's Parramatta detention centre. The gaol is now a museum and cultural centre.

'Sheep country' – a display of shearing hand-pieces at Shear Outback museum, Hay.

'Sturt's Marked Tree' – a plaque highlights explorer Charles Sturt's historic markings.

'On a nice sweeping bend of the river' – but I never did find that marked tree!

Another landmark building in Hay is that of Shear Outback. It includes the Shearers' Hall of Fame, which honours the achievements of shearers and the sheep industry. An interactive experience, a Murray Downs shearing shed and an extensive historical archive are also part of the complex. I love the display of varieties of shearing hand-pieces.

Sturt's Marked Tree is 4 kilometres east of Hay, on the Mid Western Highway. This box tree is famous for the markings which Charles Sturt carved upon it in 1829. Well, I drove out along the road from Hay to find this tree. I found the little plaque the tourist brochure mentioned, but no tree had any markings on it that I could find. I climbed the wooded stile over the fence and wandered around looking at large eucalypts in the area, to no avail. Two blokes fishing in a tinny returned to the bank downstream looking at me, but out of voice range, probably wondering what I was doing. Was I some crazy man gone bush with camera in hand? Was I a snooping Fisheries and Wildlife officer trying to photograph them with an illegal catch? Who knows, but they moved on and so did I in a vain attempt to find the Marked Tree. This place is on a nice sweeping bend of the river, where a storm seems to have bowled a few branches off the trees, including the huge one I suspect as being the tree. I return to Hay disillusioned, but vowing to return one day.

Often brochures and well-meaning tourist industry people don't check or update what they promote, and Shire officers seem too busy harassing locals about not having permits for this and that to care about some old explorer who put graffiti on a tree some 180 years ago. I find that historical societies are the best places to approach – but make sure you've got plenty of time. Most are run by retirees or ancient ladies who love to talk of the good old days.

Bless them, without their interest we'd know nothing, most young people now just don't bother to get involved.

ONE TREE HOTEL

Nearly 40 kilometres north of Hay is the One Tree Hotel. Few people realise that the current building is a replica of the original. The first One Tree pub burnt down in 1901, and the insurance claim stated that payment would only be made if the building was rebuilt exactly as the original. The only concession was that corrugated iron would cover the roof instead of wood shingles. Now the hotel is undergoing renovation work.

I first stopped to look at the outside of the One Tree Hotel in the early 1980s, when there was an old man still living there. Sadly, I didn't interview him then and he's long dead now. I've travelled up this way quite a few times since, and finally, in 2006, I saw it had been vandalised and a rough wire fence put around it, but it hadn't stopped anyone from getting in. I've yet to find the one tree though.

As I approach from the south now, I can see the hotel has a shiny new iron roof and new water tanks. The place is a construction site, with a high fence and locked gates, and there is an obvious look of rehabilitation going on. It looks like it won't be too long before it is fully restored. I have heard that at one stage they're going to pull it down and move it to Hay as part of the Shear Outback museum. I would much rather see it in its original location, on the plains where it was first built in 1862. Then called Finch's Inn, it served as a Cobb & Co staging post, where passengers stopped for lunch and a rest, while fresh horses were hitched to the coach.

Alexander Finch sold the hotel to William Clark, who also leased the huge government tank nearby, which watered up to

'Alone on wide open plains' – Col Hood took this classic shot of the hotel in the '50s.

'40 kilometres north of Hay' – Long Paddock signs welcome visitors to One Tree Hotel.

'A shiny new iron roof' – under renovation, the old pubs gets a new life in 2007.

12,000 sheep at a time. Horse and bullock teams numbering up to a thousand were watered at the charge of a penny per head. In the 1880s the McQuade family purchased the hotel until the licence lapsed in the 1940s, when it became a private residence. Although One Tree was proclaimed a village in 1885, it never grew and the pub, the sole building, now stands alone on wide open plains.

It will be interesting to see what happens when restoration is complete. It would be good to see the pub revived and made into the icon of the plains it once was. I for one would be more than happy to stop for a steak and beer.

(I've just heard it is to reopen shortly, so I am definitely off to check it out again. I have an old photograph of the pub to give the new owners that they might like to add to the wall.)

BOOLIGAL

'Oh send us to our just reward in Hay or Hell, but, precious Lord, Deliver us from Booligal.'

Banjo Paterson's poem made Booligal, 80 kilometres north of Hay, famous (or infamous). It is thought that the 'Hell' in the poem refers to Hell's Gate, a property that lies between Hay and Balranald.

On 5 July 1817 Lieutenant John Oxley RN, Surveyor-General of New South Wales, passed what was to become the village of Booligal. He and his party were the first white men to see the Riverine Plains. A monument was erected to Oxley in 1967 and remains today as a testament to his surveying of the inland river system.

Booligal was established around 1850 because it was an excellent crossing place on the Lachlan River for stock travelling from Queensland to the Darling River on the way to the major sales in Melbourne. From 1859 a punt operated across the Lachlan River to the north of the village. Edward Roset built the first bridge in Booligal in 1871–72, for which he charged a toll of threepence per wheel. This bridge was closed to traffic when another bridge was built in 1913.

The Booligal township was laid out by Surveyor Twynham and gazetted in July 1860. The first inn, the Drover's Arms, later a Cobb & Co terminus, opened in 1861. A second hotel was established in 1867 and held the name of the current hotel, the Duke of Edinburgh. The 1860s was a thriving decade for Booligal. Travellers found that the grog was plentiful at Booligal. This was because reliable sources of drink were hard to come by, with 'grog' consisting of everything from kerosene to tobacco. All drinks were sixpence, but no matter what you ordered you always got the same drink.

'First white men to see the Riverine Plains' – Booligal's memorial to John Oxley.

Today, Booligal is a tiny place, but at its height, it had two hotels, two punts, a courthouse, blacksmith, school, post office store, wool scour and several general stores. By the 1890s this town of 500 people was a centre for bullock and horse teamsters, who hauled wool and supplies as far as Willandra. In 1871 a provisional school opened, with locals applying in 1875 for it to be converted to a public school. The children were taught in a tent until a school building was erected in 1901, and it still houses local schoolchildren today. Mains electricity came to Booligal only in 1986 – at a cost of $29,000 a property – and they sealed the Cobb Highway between here and Ivanhoe in 1999.

MOSSGIEL

One house (previously the post office) is all that remains of what was once a boom town of the 1880s and a stop for Cobb & Co coaches. Besides the post office, the town had a police station, stock inspector's office and hospital – in all, there were thirty-four people dwelling here once. Hard to believe when you stop here now. The 1901 drought, an epidemic of typhoid, a mouse plague, and a lack of eggs, milk and water all had a disastrous effect on the town. After the epidemic many people who survived left the town. In 1927 a railway line from Sydney was laid through Ivanhoe, and what was Ivanhoe's gain was Mossgiel's loss. World War II saw most of the young men of the area go to war. The death knell for Mossgiel was sounded.

I am sorry to have missed interviewing Lorna Marshall, a drover/stockwoman who has lived here most of her life, except when travelling with stock on the Long Paddock. Maybe next time, Lorna.

'A born-and-bred shearer' – shearing contractor Tony 'Crowbar' Stead.

TO MANFRED STATION

VAL, PETER AND TONY 'CROWBAR' STEAD, THE SHEARING STEADS

'We used to try and get constipated so we didn't have to use station toilets.'

It is at Manfred Station, about 80 kilometres west of Mossgiel, that I catch up with owners and old friends Jock and Kerry Harris, right in the middle of the shearing season. I go there every year for a few days in the shed. I love shearing sheds. I'm also here to meet 'Crowbar' Stead, son of Val and Peter Stead, yet again.

I first met Val in the 1980s and never forgot her. She was the shearers' cook and we had a long yarn in the shearers' kitchen.

I was impressed by how hard she worked and how well organised she was, and amazed at the way she churned out lunch, dinner and tea (as well as smoko meals) for the shearers. And she didn't just chuck a heap of mash on a plate; she provided full roast meals with all the food you could eat, and followed it up with sweets. By the time the shearers were heading back to work, she was already cleaning up and preparing the next meal – everything went like clockwork. It was a hard job, but Val had been doing it for many years and knew what she needed to do. It required long hours of hard yakka in a hot, outback kitchen, just one of many she had worked in. She was easy to talk to and we yarned long over a couple of cuppas as she worked.

Her husband Peter was a long-time shearing contractor. He looked the part – a tall, sunburnt man with grey chest hair sticking out of a full woollen 'bluey' shirt with no collar, just like they wore a 100 years ago. He said it was important to keep the back warm, and full wool was the only way to go, so he always wore the shearer's bluey. I haven't seen any of the present-day shearers wearing anything similar, but Peter was one of the old school – grew up tough and worked hard all his life. A staunch union man, he fought hard for his team of shearers to make sure they got good conditions. He took no nonsense from station owners, many of whom didn't care much about the rights or needs of shearers. But Peter did.

I saw Val in the same kitchen on the same station a year or so after we first met, and we again had a good yarn. As before, there was something about this woman that really impressed me. Finally, I got to visit her and Peter at their home in Balranald on the last day of 2003 to do an interview with them both. But I was on my way home and so we agreed to continue their story when I next

'Another day – another two dollars' – a scene that could be from any shearing shed in Australia. This one is at Harts Horn, NSW.

passed through. Sadly, not long after, Val passed away from heart problems and then Peter died from bowel cancer. Their son Tony, better known as Crowbar, had worked in the shearing team and took over from his father as contractor. I see Crowbar nearly every year in the shearing shed. I heard he would be there in February 2007 for a few weeks, so I just had to add their family story.

That time in December 2003, Val talked to me in her kitchen as she made food for the family. Peter, who by then was pretty sick, was there too, and talked of the times in the early days. But I decided to interview Val first, as I knew I was coming back. I knew Peter would take a day to interview, because he had so much to tell from a lifetime of being in the shearing industry. He was an interesting man with many memories of days gone by. Some of those memories are here; the rest he took with him.

Val told me that the greatest thing as a shearers' cook was that she would 'never forget the places or the people'.

'I was born in 1934 in Balranald. Fourteen days later I returned to live on Yanga Woolshed, where my father worked as a stockman. When I went to school we rode our bikes 4 miles into town and then home again. By the time I was eight we'd moved into town to live. I did all my schooling in Balranald and then worked for the local chemist. Peter and I married in 1956. We've got three boys – all shearers: Michael, who's forty-seven, Tony, forty-five, and Russell, forty-two. Our daughter Bronwyn, forty, is a hairdresser in town. We've got four grandchildren.

'In 1979, it was a very wet year. Bronwyn had just left school. We put on two teams of shearers, but because of the wet we couldn't get the sheds finished. Peter said to me, "You'll have to come and cook for me." I thought I'd finish in about three or four months when the run finished, but it just went on from there. I loved it. The first shed I worked at was Duckshot, 30 miles from Oxley, owned by Mrs Joan Ryall, a widow. We worked her place every year until she died. Usually about 6000 sheep to shear.

'When I first went there, there were brand-new quarters, new lino on the floor. In the kitchen were two new gas stoves, lovely big fridges, but no power. The electric motor from the shearing shed had to be started each morning first thing. I'd be up at 5.30 am and cook breakfast for the team – chops, sausages, bacon, eggs, tomatoes, spaghetti and toast for twelve people. The shearing team consisted of shearers, shed-hand, wool-classer, wool-presser, contractor. Breakfast was at 6.30 am. Then I'd wash up everything before doing anything else. Then I'd start smoko, which the men had at 9.30 am, and it consisted of sandwiches, cakes, biscuits, and in winter it was sausage rolls, scones, pancakes – just something hot. Smoko was for half an hour. After I cleaned up it was time to get the vegetables ready for lunch. Lunch was either cold meat or roast meat, chops, cutlets, whatever meat supply you had. Lunch went from 12 to 1 pm.

'After lunch I'd wash up and get ready for the afternoon half-hour smoko, which was at 3 pm. Then I'd wash up and get ready for tea, which was at 6.30 pm. Tea was soup – you always had to have soup – followed by a full roast meat or cold meat. And sweets. Before electricity arrived I even used to make homemade ice-cream. One shearer said to me when I made it one day, "I want ice-cream every day." So I used to make it from carnation milk. Tea was 6.30 to 7.30 pm. I'd be washed up and out of the kitchen by 7.45. Sometimes in winter they'd all play cards, but mostly everyone just went to bed early. Five days a week, Monday to Friday.

'I used to take out all the food to last a week, and we'd come home at weekends and order the next week's lot of food. Bread also came out on the mail truck twice a week. In all our time we never went outside the shire – we had enough sheds to work. Twenty years after, frozen foods became available, and packed meat and milk. I supplied newspapers and magazines for the shearers. I always tried to do my best. I always had the best meat – lamb, plus other meat like mince. Corn was a favourite. Originally I had to use a kerosene refrigerator, and later it was gas, and then for twenty-odd years it was electric. Before long-life milk or electricity, we had to have two big tins of powdered milk. For twelve men for the week, I would buy two big boxes of long-life milk, twenty loaves of bread, 50 pounds of potatoes. I always cooked more in winter. It was a bit different in the 1950s – cooks would throw food out. Kitchens always supplied, but baking dishes didn't fit or a boiler was too small or too big, so I supplied a lot myself. I used all my own, plastic containers. I took my own as then I knew I had them. I even took my own fan.

'Most of the kitchens were pretty good. I loved the old wood stoves. You had to watch which way the wind blew, though, or you could end up with a lot of smoke. They were lovely old stoves to use. I always did my purchases in our local grocery at Balranald. We had a three-month account; he'd even send me stuff from the hardware store if I needed anything.'

I sensed that in the early days it was tough work, and much easier now. Mind you, having seen how hard the shearers' cooks still work, I reckon they do a marvellous job.

'In the early days, you did more things like go outside to get water,' Val continued. 'You'd fill a bucket from the tank and carry it back, boil it on the stove. There was no fly-wire on the doors, just meat safes to keep flies off the food. Some places in the early days were shocking. The heat of a kitchen in February out here was pretty bad, especially without electricity or fans.

'A lot of the time the beds were outside, as it was too hot inside the shearers' quarters. Sometimes you'd wake every hour or so to keep the dust off the bed. In the morning often you could get up and see the imprint in dust of where you'd laid the night before. I'd have to be up early to sweep the dust out of the kitchen and wipe dust off the breakfast table, before I even started work. Dust kept rolling in every day. I remember when for four weeks at Hart's Horn near Ivanhoe it was never below 100°F the whole time. I had a wet towel on my shoulders the whole time I was there. Between smokos, I used to sleep with a wet towel over my whole body just to keep a bit cooler. I'd walk through the kitchen and dirty footprints were left on the floor wherever I walked. All fourteen men were sleeping outside; now every room has double adapters and air-conditioners.

'I always had rules for my shearers,' says Val. 'They didn't come to meals without a shirt on, their feet had to be covered, and there was no bad language.

'Later I bought myself a four-wheel drive. I got sick of being bogged all the time.

'I got very niggly when I had to retire due to having had a heart by-pass operation. I really hated it when they'd go off and leave me at home. It took a while to adjust.'

Before I got back to interview Val and Peter again, Val died suddenly from a heart attack. Within four months, Peter had succumbed also to the cancer he had fought for some time. In some ways it seemed appropriate they went close together – they had spent a lifetime together, and worked for many years in shearing across the stations of the Balranald district and beyond.

I rechecked some old notes and found some comments by Peter.

'I was born at Wilcannia on the Darling in 1935. My parents both died when I was young. I grew up in Balranald. I started work as a boundary rider first, but in 1950 I went into the shearing business, first as a rouseabout at Glendee, up Oxley Road. Then in 1954 I started shearing myself and crutching. As a boundary rider I was earning £5 10s a week. Rouseabout wages were lousy – I got 10 shillings a day. Then as a shearer I was getting £5 2s 6d for every 100 sheep I shore. We also worked Saturday morning.

'My heart was always set on shearing. My first memories of shearing in 1953–54 was that a lot the properties were really big; now most are all cut up into smaller places. When I started, all the shearers would jump on the back of a truck with their swag and off we'd go. We'd be picked up on Sunday afternoon and go off to a shed, which usually lasted about three or four weeks of shearing. We'd go out and stay there until the shed finished – very few shearers had cars.

'The only differences now are electricity and the power press and wide combs. Nothing much else changed. Sheds were better then. Fifty years later and there's never been much money spent on the sheds, some are falling down. Some of the sheds, the Lachlan sheds for instance, were bloody beautiful. Duckshot – an unbelievable shed. Korong was a beautiful old shed – everything was mortised timber. In the old days, the bigger the shed the better they were. Sheep were penned out of the weather underneath; the toilets were better.

'But generally the toilets at most sheds in the '50s were bloody awful. God, that was the worst set-up, the toilets in the 1950s. Hart's Horn got nice new septics when the wind blew over the old dunny. Now, with septics, handbasins and water, it's good.

'Dysentery would break out in many sheds prior to getting septic systems. They'd put two drops of chloradine into the water to stop dysentery when it broke out. We'd all try and get constipated so we didn't have to go to the toilets. A bucket of sheep dip was often used to clean the toilets and bathroom. Often there'd be no toilet paper, only disinfectant. I'd always say, "Talk to the people" – the farmers usually understood. All we wanted as workers was a bit of consideration. Some farmers were tough – it was pretty hard generally speaking in the 1950s and '60s, but things gradually got better. Old kapok mattresses, often wet or torn, were gradually replaced by rubber mattresses.

'The main things a shearer needs are a good bed, hot water, good meals and a good cook. With a good cook you got harmony. They're professional cooks now compared to the old days. "One snap of a twig and off they'd go" – the older cooks years ago were very touchy.

'I was shearing for about ten to twelve years, then in 1968 I took on being a shearing contractor. I'd shorn with a contractor, Ted Joliffe, for a long time. He had sons and came to me one day and asked me to take over the run. He lent me some dollars to cover workers' compensation insurance. I had a young family so I took it on. We worked most months of the year – three months shearing and crutching just one shed, that's how big they were back then. We were shearing about 4000 sheep a week. I remember one place was called Ioana. Edgar Nicholson was the owner. When he told his son he'd called it Ioana, his son said, "Why? What do you mean, Dad?" Edgar replies, "I own her" – the farm. So it became known as Ioana.

'When the wide combs issue arose, I was contracting on Oxley Station. The dispute split up the job – some wanted wide combs, some didn't. I thought it would all blow over, but on the Thursday I flew to Narrandera for a union meeting and it was three days off. Start Wednesday, they said, but by Monday, no. I lost a shed over it, the owner not happy. He waited another two weeks to get another contractor. I always stuck by my men. The men asked, "What are we going to do?" I said, "whatever you want" – eventually they went to wide combs shearing. For a few weeks, there were a few hard feelings; some of the men went to other teams. Some of the hardliners said, "I've shore all my life with narrow combs and I'm not changing now." I thought it wouldn't make much difference – forget it and get on with it. All shearers were good, some were just quicker than others.

'Shearers are the most honestly paid workers there are. They get paid for the work that they do: shear 100 sheep, get paid for 100 sheep. The rouseabouts are the worst off the union is piss weak. I told them I stuck up for rousies, but they are still worse off.

'There was never a shortage of shearers, but graziers always want the contractor in the same month. We knew in January where we'd be working in December. At one stage I had three or four and even five teams of shearers working at once. Then I went back to one or two teams – it was better financially, as I knew what was going on more.'

Anyone who talks to a shearer wants to know how many sheep he can shear in a day, so naturally I had to ask Peter.

'In 1962 on the east coast of Tasmania I shore 276 in one day. But Tony Birch of Longreach still beat me – he shore 306.'

Val cuts in to tell me that on his last day of shearing (and his sixty-fifth birthday) Peter shore at Hart's Horn shed and did 200 sheep for the day. I don't think Peter was going to mention that.

'Funny how you remember things. When I was leaving Tasmania in 1963 to come home, I saw a bloke sitting in the gutter crying. I was walking to catch a taxi and when I asked what was wrong he replied, "They shot President Kennedy."

'I gave shearing away between '66 and '67, saying I'll go back when they pay $20 a hundred. I worked as a barman at the Shamrock Hotel, but was back shearing the next year and then contracting again.

'I never took shearing jobs in other areas – it'd mean someone in that area would miss out on work, and that wasn't on as far as I was concerned. In the early days we worked on just five properties between Balranald and Ivanhoe: Paik, D Block, Till Till, Clare and Manfred [Hart's Horn]. Now there are probably 150 properties, ranging from 20 to 33,000 acres.'

It was here my notes end with 'To be continued', as I intended to interview Peter and Val again on my next trip north. It was the end of the year and I wanted to get home that day, so I left them. It would be the last time I saw them. I shall always remember them both.

It's February 2007 and I'm back at Hart's Horn shearing shed, where Tony 'Crowbar' Stead and his shearing team are into day four of the first of two shearing dates on the property this year. Hart's Horn is 41,000 acres and part of Manfred Station, 54,000 acres owned by Jock and Kerry Harris. Next to that is Melton Grove, whose 50,000 acres are owned by Jock's mother. And adjoining it, Jock and Kerry have recently bought another 116,000 acres called Mulurulu. They can travel across a quarter of a million acres of dirt and grass and not leave their own land.

Ben Chaffey owned Manfred Station in the 1920s when, on its own, it was over 1 million acres. Many of the stations he owned still exist, but most have now been cut up into smaller ones.

Ben Chaffey – 'the Kidman of Sheep' – once owned many stations along the Darling. He dreamed of owning over twenty stations up and down the country so that he could always have land somewhere that was free of drought. His father George and uncle Ben were the founders of the Murray River Irrigation Scheme at Mildura and Renmark. When you drive from Mildura into New South Wales you cross the George Chaffey Bridge. I could write a book on Ben Chaffey. I followed his life in great detail both here and in America, interviewing many people associated with him. I worked and did a lot of the history research at a historic home, Woodlands, once owned by him. It's near Melbourne's Tullamarine Airport and is now a historic park run by Parks Victoria.

Ben Chaffey was a man ahead of his time. He took all his stockmen off horseback and put them into T-model Ford utes; he installed private phone lines to outstations on many of his properties; and pipelines took water to far-off areas of his land to make them drought-proof long before other landholders did the same. The New South Wales Railways even installed a rail siding just to carry his sheep and wool and supplied him with carriages.

In 1926 Manfred Station sheared 102,000 sheep, and had 260 employees. I interviewed one of the station's employees years ago. I tracked down countless photographs and private Chaffey items, including furniture and his gold watch, which had been scattered to his friends over the years. I even interviewed the man who melted down the Caulfield Cup that one of Chaffey's horses won ('Manfred', named after the property, was one of his famous racehorses). One lady, who was in her late eighties when I interviewed her in the 1980s, recalled travelling with him and his daughter Mavis in his chauffeur-driven Rolls-Royce to numerous stations on inspection. Ben kept the Rolls and the chauffeur right up until the day he died, even though his fortune disappeared due to drought and the Great Depression. His brother Andrew went on to build a large banking chain in America that remains in business to this day.

I keep telling Jock Harris that he is 'doing a Chaffey', buying more and more land, but he informs me that they 'aren't in the market for any more stations'.

Well, I add the word 'yet'.

'Doing a Chaffey' – multiple station owner Jock Harris deep in thought.

Crowbar Stead comes to Manfred for tea that night and we share some memories across the table with the family. All have spent many years dealing with the shearing Steads. Out come the photographs of the good old days. Jock and Kerry's boys Ryan, Rhys and Zack are home, but the other two, Dallas and Leon, are not here. Jane is in England. It is a busy time. There are 12,000 sheep to be shorn in the next week or so. Then Crowbar and his team will be gone, only to come back in September. Melton Grove, Jock's mother's place, will be shorn as part of Crowbar's run of properties. And now Jock and Kerry's new station, Mulurulu, will be added to the list.

First I want to know how Crowbar got his nickname.

'Well, it was mainly because as a young kid I was as skinny as a crowbar and the name stuck. Of course, a few other reasons have been told over the years in the shearing sheds. One yarn was because I had won a crowbar-throwing competition, and another was that I was hung like a crowbar,' he says with a big grin and a laugh.

'The new shearing Steads' – Russell, Jarryd and Tony.

Crowbar sucks on a handle of whisky and I soon learn the ins and outs of this family business. Times are tough, and the drought is affecting the business like everyone else's. Crowbar has a team of sixteen working for him – a bit different to when he employed sixty. He still has work ten months of the year around the properties, though.

Crowbar was born in 1958 and is a tall rangy bloke like his dad. He is married to Tracy, who is a postal clerk in Balranald. He left school in Balranald in 1973 and first worked as a jackaroo for twelve months on Bunumburt, south of Oxley. At the age of seventeen, he first went shearing with his parents as a rouseabout for about eight months. He was taught to shear by his father in 1975 and stayed until 1977, before going to Adelaide to work for racehorse trainer Ted Cameron as a stable-hand for six years. He travelled with horses to Melbourne, Sydney and Brisbane and was based at Swan Hill until 1983.

'In 1983 I returned home to work with shearing again and am still doing it. I took over as a shearer contractor from Dad in 1994. Dad was sixty-five and ready to retire. My brother Michael shore with Dad but he doesn't shear now, he's a general hand at Hillston. Russell, my other brother, shears on my team and has done so since 1996. My son Leighton, nineteen is a rouseabout, and my nephew Jarryd, eighteen, is wool-presser for the team.

'When I took over as contractor from Dad I had many of his old sheds to shear, but in that first year I was also asked to shear on Yanga Station for the first time – 45,000 sheep. It was a big step up for me to walk into being a contractor, and especially taking on Yanga as well.'

Yanga is one of the big old sheds near Balranald. Crowbar's mother Val grew up there. The property was bought by the state government and given to National Parks and local Aborigines. No longer is it an operational shearing shed. Crowbar and his team were the last to shear there.

'A shearer friend went to have a walk down the shed and see all the stands, well over twenty, just to get a feel for it, but they have now wired it all up and you can't even get into the shed. Such a sad waste of a great shed.

'Yanga not shearing sheep is sad. We shore 45,000 sheep there each year. We employed sixty people and shore there for three months. When I started on my own as a contractor we did Manfred, Springdale, Tylden, Waldaira, Bunumburt, Glendee, Duckshot and Thelangerin.

Now in 2007, Crowbar and the Stead team shear sheep at Manfred (Hart's Horn shed), Bluebush, Waldaira, Tylden, Kungie, Cringadale, Hazelwood, Springdale, Bunumburt,

'With a good cook you get harmony' – Karen Jones brings morning smoko at Hart's Horn.

Minarto, Alma, Thelangerin, Lake Marimley, Auley, Fedla, Melton Grove, Neila … As for the rest, Crowbar is scratching his head. 'Think that's it,' he says.

'At one stage Mum and Dad had twice as many sheds as I have now, they were flat out twelve months of the year, one as a crutching team. Now we have ten months shearing and employ twelve on a regular basis, but up to sixteen. We've had several cooks since Mum gave it away, but now Karen Jones is our regular cook. She's pretty good.'

He wouldn't have been game to say if she was better than his mum Val.

'The sheds Dad did included The Vale, Round Plain, Orange Grove, Hart's Horn, Melton Grove, Ettrick, Glen Emu, Springdale, Glendee, Tylden, Bunumburt, Oxley Station, Jermaney, Topuntal, Brass But, Duckshot, Thelangerin, Darcoola,

Torry Plains, Willowvale, Jeraly, Waldaira, Paika, Min Min, The Ridge, Carinya – if I look back through the tally books probably there'd be more as well.'

What are the changes in the shearing industry? I ask him.

'It's a lot harder now. Wool prices dropped but wages increased. OH&S [Occupational Health and Safety] issues – shearing is the last industry in the workforce to have it, it's made everyone more aware. Commonsense should prevail. Dad always impressed upon me about the importance of it. Rules changed a lot, and awards. Dad was known as "Placid Pete" – he was casual but he'd let you know if things were wrong. Give him a fair go and he was OK. I remember one bloke saying to me when I started, "If you run your show like your old man you'll do all right."

'Unfortunately OH&S is costing the industry. I've already had two people claim from the system. There's more money being paid out in the industry on OH&S than is being paid in. My insurance policies go up, I have to pay excesses, and it all cuts into your profits. It is way out of hand. The ongoing costs are getting harder. I've been at it fifteen years as a contractor and the longer I am in it the dearer it gets. Workers' compensation is the real big killer. WorkCare has destroyed the industry.

'Now, too, everyone wants it yesterday. In the old days you worked down the line and got to your shed when it was your time – now they all want it done yesterday. Also it's harder to get young shearers; they are hard to find. Shed-hands and rousies are OK, but they don't want to go on shearing. The average age now for a shearer is forty years old. Having a trade means they can do more things work-wise and closer to home. Shearing still takes you away from home, although many drive home if it's not too far away. Most, though, don't go home until Friday afternoon.

'The most honestly paid workers' – hard yakka in the shearing shed.

'Shearing still takes you away from home' – have ute, will travel.

'Electricity, the power press and wide combs' – changes all the way down the line.

'Drought is affecting the business' – Manfred wool.

'Each worth three men' – it's a dog's life rounding up sheep.

'Work until exhaustion' – canine takes a smoko.

'I'd love to keep it all going, but it is getting harder. Shearers now get $200 per 100 sheep shorn. They work from 7.30 am to 9.30 am then have half an hour off for smoko, before the second run, which goes from 10 am to 12 noon; then one hour for lunch, then the third run is 1 pm to 3 pm, and a half-hour smoko; and then the final and fourth run is 3.30 pm to 5.30 pm. An average shearer would do 140 sheep a day. My six shearers would do 1000 a day on average. There's always a gun shearer – one who does more. My gun bloke here did 196 for the day yesterday. It is a bit easier using wide combs now, everyone in the industry uses wide combs.'

Crowbar is a born-and-bred shearer, and somehow I can't see him doing anything else. His son and nephew are the next generation to carry it on, and and with Val and Peter having four grandchildren something tells me there will be more shearing Steads for years to come.

'At the end of my days, if I can see it out shearing 120 a day I'd be happy. My back isn't as good as it was, and over all if I'd just been shearing all my life and nothing else I'd still be better off.'

I'm up early next morning, to have breakfast with Jock and Kerry before the work day begins. Early morning in western New South Wales is a nice time of day, like the evenings. The dogs are barking in anticipation of going on the utes to round up sheep or work in the yards and shearing shed. They are each worth three men, these dogs on the land. At the shed I go around and pat all of them – Jock's dogs, Crowbar's dogs, and even the shearers have their own dogs with them. Whoever coined the phrase 'Dogs are man's best friend' must have seen these animals at work on farms. Dogs and men go together like men and sheds (especially if there's a ute in the shed as well). All dogs will work until exhaustion to please man, and a cool clean drink of water and a good pat for a job well done is all they want – as well as good tucker. They are the world's most loyal animals.

For me it's time to pack and look to the track again. I will soon be off the dirt road and into Ivanhoe, and then back on dirt to Wilcannia. But I get ahead of myself.

KILFERA STATION

I drive past another property en route to Ivanhoe, one that I've stayed at once before, although I don't have time to call in today. Next time, Clive. Kilfera was another of Ben Chaffey's properties back in the 1920s. Kilfera is now owned by Clive Linnet, his wife Faye and son Peter. I stayed in the shearers' quarters years ago. The Linnets are responsible for the annual field day event on their property, which attracts hundreds of people from hundreds of kilometres away. The field day displays stock and farming equipment, but it is also an important social event. The Linnets do a great job organising the field day to raise money for charity.

When I stayed with the Linnets, Clive showed me around and through the original old homestead, built in the 1800s. While lived in for many, many decades, it was then no longer in use. I have photos of it in my collection. The old homestead was right next door to the Linnets' new home. It was lucky I had a look through the old homestead when I did, because it was destroyed on 30 September 1998 in a freak accident. At 11 am that day, a Piper Cherokee aeroplane, which had left Jamestown, South Australia, for the Kilfera field day, tried to land at the station. It had to abort the landing, probably because of strong winds, and the left wing of the aircraft struck a tall radio mast. The aircraft rolled to the left, passed through the branches of a large tree, turned upside down and crashed into the ground. Both the pilot and his passenger were killed, and the fire that subsequently broke out spread to the old homestead and razed it.

There was, long ago, another big fire at Kilfera. Back in 1892, during the shearers' strike, Kilfera became embroiled in controversy, and the shearing shed was burnt down by striking shearers.

IVANHOE

As I drive into town a sign says 'Ivanhoe: the Southern Cross Town'. It immediately attracts my attention as I haven't noticed it before. Since when did Ivanhoe become the Southern Cross town? I wonder – and why?

Seems few people in the town know the full history, although at the local post office I do gain some information. The best person to talk to, apparently, has moved to Adelaide, but someone graciously tracks down the phone number and rings me a few days later. Obliging folk. Another in the shop says I should contact another person. No answer. No brochures. Now, I'm not going to let this one slip. I want to know and I intend to find out. I'm an inquisitive bastard and, like a dog on a bone, I'm not going to let go until I've finished.

Finally, I get to have a phone interview with Jenny Farrer, way down at the end of the Murray River. It turns out that she's the instigator of the Southern Cross town idea. 'It was about five years ago at a town meeting. I was put in charge of the beautification of the streets in Ivanhoe, which was a bit of a task for sure. Anyway, I had an idea and I rang the Mount Stromlo Observatory near Canberra and asked them, whether there were any stars related in any way whatsoever to Ivanhoe or the outback, or something we could put our name to. A couple of days later someone rang back and said no, there was nothing at all that she could relate to us in some way. We were talking, and out of the blue I asked her, "What about the Southern Cross?" She said no one had ever asked to buy a whole constellation, but when she checked she found no one had, and so we paid, I think, $1400 for the naming rights to the Southern Cross stars. Purely a chance. No one owns the stars, of course, but you can buy the rights to use them like we are now.'

I comment on how, apart from the sign on the edge of town, there is nothing else to explain how or why. Jenny replies: 'Unfortunately I think, with the drought being so bad now, people have more important things to worry about, but hopefully they will proceed further with it. There's a small telescope there in town [sorry Jenny, but I missed it!], and there's talk of doing more. There's also four or five cylinders set up in the shape of the Southern Cross and more stuff planned.'

As Jenny is now living a long way from Ivanhoe, her input won't be like it was, but at least she came up with the idea. Now it is up to Ivanhoe to live up to the name and make something spectacular happen.

The Southern Cross stars are my own logo for 'The Uteman', so I have a special feeling towards this constellation. I have lain in my swag many, many times looking at the stars that make it up. You never feel alone in the outback when looking at it. Often my wife looks up at it at night, at home in the backyard, knowing I may be many hundreds or thousands of kilometres away but doing the same thing as she is – looking at the Southern Cross. It is our own special little way of reaching out and being together when far apart.

People are fascinated with the stars and get romantic about them. I even know a lovely Westpac teller called Aurora. Not sure if she is named after Aurora australis or borialis or whatever. Will we see names like Jennifer Southern Cross, or Billy Cow Jumped Over the Moon, or Mary Super Nova, or Mike Haleys Comet? There are even sillier names out there already. 'Aurora' sounds nice, though.

I want to see Ivanhoe do something brilliant and captivating and make you want to go to the town to see something special created around the theme of the Southern Cross. Calling the place 'Ivanhoe: the Southern Cross Town' on a street sign just isn't enough. Apparently Southern Cross windmills have agreed to assist with a display of their products. I hope people don't get confused and think that the windmill company started in Ivanhoe! Anyway, a heap of windmills as a display set in the shape of the stars would look good photographed from the air. C'mon all you Ivanhoe-ites and surrounding landowners – make your town the best advertisement for our wonderful constellation. I for one will return to your town to see it.

North of Ivanhoe, I reach the intersection of the Cobb and Barrier highways. Behind us are a lot of kilometres of the Long Paddock road. I have left out on purpose some of the stops along the way. You need to go see it all yourself and experience a different land. It is really just the first stage of our trip.

Turn left at the intersection and it's about a kilometre into Wilcannia.

WILCANNIA

Wilcannia is at the end of the Long Paddock – 610 kilometres from Echuca.

What a sad place it is. I've been through it and around it many times. Very rarely do you find many people on the streets. Residents stay indoors, and most of the shops are barricaded with iron bars on all windows. Doors remain closed. The large corner store has all of its broken windows now permanently covered with sheets of second-hand corrugated iron and painted with red, yellow and black graffiti. The service station is always open and you will see the occasional visitor stopping for petrol or supplies. Most people simply don't stop here. It is an example of poor Australia. Reconciliation doesn't seem to have come to Wilcannia yet.

Wilcannia has had a long history, though. Sturt, Burke and Wills, and others explored this country, and a few nice old buildings remain from the early days of settlement.

TO WAVE OR NOT TO WAVE

There's a very odd thing been happening in the outback roads and across the Nullarbor and other long-haul trips for a long time. For instance, if you drive from Broken Hill to Wentworth or vice versa, people travelling in the opposite direction to you will wave casually at you almost without a shadow of a doubt, but only for the first 180 kilometres south of The Hill, then they stop waving because now you are nearer to civilisation. If you travel from Wentworth up to Broken Hill it is the same once you are at least 20 kilometres from Wentworth. Most people wave. Is this a silent but recognised acknowledgement of your efforts? Are they saying, 'Good onya mate, you're heading outback', or 'Good onya mate, you've been outback and survived it, now we're heading off to do the same'? There are exceptions to the rule. People who drive Mercedes, Saabs, Audis and the like seem to think they don't have to; for them, it is obviously something that 'other' people do.

Some truckies won't, or are slow to wave back. I guess being on the road all day every day, if they waved to everyone they'd have bloody RSI of the index finger. There are different types of wavers, too. Some flip one finger off the steering wheel skywards at you, others use two or more fingers or a whole hand. Sometimes even the passenger will join in. The best ones at it are caravaners. When you tow a caravan, it seems like every bloody caravan driver and passenger has nothing better to do than wave to other caravaners, in a general salute to say, 'Howdy … Yep, we're free on the road too – great, isn't it?' Sometimes this strange but wonderful mob go further and flash their headlights, or get on the CB/UHF for a chat. They even put their names and channel on the back of their vans for all to see. Things like 'Des & Doreen Channel 18'. Some get fancy and write names like 'The Happy Wanderers', or 'Bill & Betty, Grey Nomads', or 'Fred and Myrtle – Spending the Kids' Inheritance'. All sorts of tags.

Some city people just don't understand. I remember when a convoy of twelve blokes and six utes were travelling from Sydney to Perth for a ute show. One bloke from Sydney got in beside me after we'd been swapping drivers and passengers around. When we started off he said to me, 'Did you know Mongrel waves to every bloody car or truck that goes by?' When I explained it was just part of the unspoken road law on remote or long drives in outback areas, he seemed puzzled, and even more so when I spent the next couple of hours doing the same thing as Mongrel, who is a bushie like me. The other bloke was from Sydney (what would you expect?), where they only use one-finger waves – and it isn't to say hello!

The Nullarbor is one of those roads where most people wave, even truckies. Not that there's as many truckies going across like they used to. Now, most of the goods go by huge freight trains, sometimes a couple of kilometres long, carrying hundreds of shipping containers. Cheaper to have just a few train drivers than to be paying hundreds of truckies. Caravanning people will drive you bananas on the Nullarbor if you don't like to wave. There are hundreds of them, like ants swarming along a track.

Me, I like waving. It is a peaceful pasttime, makes you feel people are friendly after all, and it doesn't cost anything. Mongrel and I have a rule: you wave and if they don't wave back as they fly past you, then you finish the wave off with a one-fingered gesture aimed to the sky.

Sadly, the Long Paddock road doesn't see many people waving for some reason. Maybe they are just stupefied by the long open plains. As for those toffs who think their car is too good to be soiled by waving to people on the road: stuff yas. A car doesn't make you any better than the rest of us enjoying life on the roads of Oz.

Northwards, and it is getting hotter by the minute.

'Overlooking the dusty opal town' – Margaret Anne 'Ma' Baker, White Cliffs.

WHITE CLIFFS TO BOURKE

MARGARET ANNE 'MA' BAKER, AN OUTBACK OPAL

'It's my spirit place.'

On this trip from Wilcannia to White Cliffs it is hot. Bloody hot – 47.3°C! A further 93 kilometres and I am looking forward to the cool 22°C underground in the opal dugout built by Allenby Stuchbery in the 1970s. Although from Bendigo, Allenby and his family often made their way here, particularly Allenby. He retired to the dugout called Eagle's Nest, high on Turleys Hill and overlooking the dusty opal town.

Allenby died and nowadays the dugout is home to his daughter, Anne, known as Ma. I've known the family for some

'From Turleys Hill' – looking back to White Cliffs, solar panels on the horizon (left).

years now. I first came to White Cliffs with Bluey, son of Allenby and Margaret. On that trip I also got to see White Cliffs from the air. This local bloke, Graham, owns his own aeroplane and he took me flying so that I could photograph the diggings and town from the air. He didn't say so but I soon found out that once in the air, he wanted to see if he could make me sick! He threw the aeroplane around like he was in an air derby, twisting this way and that. I casually continued to photograph and not bat an eye. The harder he tried, the more I ignored his efforts.

Eventually, he gave up and his flying returned to a more normal manner. What he didn't know (and I never told him) was that I had been flying since the 1970s, when I learnt on Cessnas and spent a lot of time upside down in a Tiger Moth that belonged to a mate. Sorry, Graham – I think I've only been sick in a plane twice over many years of flying. Once I was in a glider that had no air flowing into the stinking-hot cockpit, and we were doing spirals; the other time was when I was a kid on a very rough flight from Melbourne to Broken Hill.

White Cliffs is 290 kilometres northeast of Broken Hill and 90-odd kilometres north of Wilcannia. Localities on the opal fields here, like Potch Gully, Golden Gully, Somebodys, Everybodys, Nobodys and The Londoner, all have that outback feel to them. White Cliffs has less tourism than Coober Pedy, and a more settled look than Andamooka, but the town's architecture is not as interesting as Lightning Ridge's.

The last time I was on the road to White Cliffs was when I was coming from Broken Hill and at the time I was not feeling very happy. My old mate Pro Hart had just told me he had motor neurone disease. Things weren't looking good, and I knew I'd seen my mate for the last time. My mind was elsewhere. I actually bought some sandwiches and a drink at an isolated Little Topar roadhouse and left without paying. Half an hour up the road I remembered and had to drive back to pay.

This time I head into town from the Wilcannia road. Driving through town I finally arrive at Eagle's Nest, where I am greeted by Ma, Bluey's sister. This is her story.

If I said Ma rode a Harley-Davidson motorbike, was a state champion javelin thrower, lives underground in a dugout with two dogs, plays a mean banjo, and that her four-wheel drive ute is called 'the Urban Assault Vehicle', you'd probably reckon she is a candidate for the title of ... interesting character.

Well, Ma Baker comes from a family of 'doers'. Ma enjoys life out here and is taking a long sabbatical from being a kindergarten teacher.

A woman alone in the outback has to contend with what life throws at her, and Ma takes it all in her own way. She had a major operation on her knee earlier this year and part of her therapy is to go play a bit of golf at 6 am.

Next day, and by 9 am it's 40°C with a hot wind. Ma is suffering from the effects of a late-night street party. She hit her bed about 3.30 am. I was under the air-conditioner a couple of hours earlier, after having had a few beers with some new-found friends at the pub and out in the hot street after midnight.

It was an OK night; if being in the heat listening to half-drunks on a karaoke machine is what cranks your engine. Me, I'd rather have heard a real band playing – and they blew up the karaoke machine. Aren't they one of the world's worst inventions? Invented for the worst singers known to man but who think they have talent.

But it was good to meet some interesting new people and relax.

Yesterday it reached 47.7°C; today it is 47°C and climbing. Even the air-conditioner is breathing hard. I wash out some shirts and jeans and they dry in about ten minutes hanging over a branch of a small peppercorn. I probably don't look my best just in my boots, socks and jocks but I'm hidden away, overlooking the town from Turleys Hill. Ma is underground somewhere resting in the cool darkness of one of the rooms off the main tunnel. A solitary ute is driving across the flat plain to the back of town, a line of dust trailing behind, which hangs in the air for a long time.

The driver, I assume, is like a retreating animal in the heat, making its way to a cooler abode somewhere out in the desert, where an underground opal mine is home and a cool respite from the stifling heat. People ask me why I go into the outback at the hottest time of the year. I reply that as a writer I want to experience it in all its seasons.

'47°C and climbing' – the entrance to Ma Baker's cool underground haven.

Later on, while Ma still lies in the dark room, I sit in the nearby lounge room interviewing her. Her voice echoes from within the dark room out to where I sit with the two dogs. First time I've ever interviewed someone who's not in the same room as me.

Ma is divorced with grown-up children and is experiencing a different lifestyle. She is a good organiser and will turn her hand to anything. She's done a course on GST accounts management, but she can use a jackhammer to blast through a stone rock-face in the opal country and get covered in powder-like dust from head to foot.

But how did this woman end up out here on her own?

Ma grew up in central Victoria with her three brothers. She learnt to be independent from an early age; her parents made sure of it. By the time she was eleven years old, she easily won a competition by throwing a softball the farthest. Her sports-mad father saw the potential in her. She wasn't allowed to compete in some sports because she was too young, so her father trained her up ready for competition. At the tender age of thirteen she won the Victorian senior country javelin title in the open age group. The following year she won the state junior under-sixteen title and also won the state under-eighteen title. She held the state record for javelin with a throw of, according to Ma, '115 feet – and quarter of an inch'.

All of her family were sports minded. Her mother, Margaret, started the South Bendigo Women's Athletic Club, and even in his later years her father held the pole-vaulting record for veterans. As her mother had previously said to me, 'We lived at the sports ground practically, training about three times a week. Then competitions at the weekend, and they even came around to our house for practice. Shot put, javelin, discus throwing and hammer.'

At one point, Ma had to choose between swimming and athletics. She went with athletics.

'Dad trained me. Dad and Mum wouldn't let me train in Melbourne. I came fifth in the National Titles in Melbourne one year. Sport has always been a big part of my life. Later on I went to Bendigo Teachers' College and qualified as a primary teacher in 1968. All through college I competed in sports. I did things like waterskiing, netball, archery, canoeing. Also I did basketball and hockey, both as a player and an umpire right up until about five years ago. I was always keen to try different things. Horses scared me a bit, though. I was good at tenpin bowling and was always playing it in inter-college competitions.'

Ma had no physical problems in her athletic career, but eventually required a major knee operation (her first) in 2004. As part of her recovery strategy, she plays golf, carpet and outdoor bowls, and does water aerobics to regain strength.

'We have a little pool in White Cliffs and I used to go in at 6.45 every morning, but I've only been three times this last month. I swim twice a week if I go to Bendigo, though. Carpet bowls is every Wednesday, and that's good. I will soon get back to more aerobics. I also walked down the hill from here to town to the mailbox, but it's a bitch walking uphill home. And, of course, jackhammering keeps you fit,' she laughs. 'I did jogging right up until about five years ago. To get my fitness back up I went on an 8-kilometre hike last week at Parnoo-Darling National Park at Peery Lake.'

I want to know more of Ma's early life and so we back-track a bit.

After she qualified as a primary school teacher in 1968, she did a year teaching at Ultima and then two years at Chewton. In 1971 she met Ian Baker through a friend.

'He had a ski-boat they skied behind. He was a carpenter and joiner. We were married in 1971 and we took off to work around Australia. We had a 1969 Holden car and a new caravan. We first worked on the Gold Coast. Ian was fitting out a new motel and I was a waitress in a Chinese restaurant. Then we wandered up the coast and finally into Mount Isa, where Ian got a job doing formwork for Thiess Bros and I worked in a dress shop. Ian later worked for Jennings as a building subcontractor, and later I ended up working as a teacher at St Joseph's. We stayed there for two years. By then I was pregnant with Matthew [born in 1974], so we came home to Bendigo. Ian worked as a subcontract builder and I was working as a physical education teacher at St Mary's – until they found out I was pregnant.

'I decided to improve my qualifications with the Education Department, so I did more study at teachers' college, and Kirstin

'The Urban Assault Vehicle' – Ma Baker's ute.

was born in 1976. By 1978 I was preschool teaching for eight years at Heathcote and studying so I could do both primary and kindergarten. Dual qualifications. Finally, I ended up with a degree in teaching.'

Ian and Anne divorced in 1983. She bought a house in Spring Gully, and worked from 1986 to 2000 at Marong Pre-School, near Bendigo. She still owns a home at Lockwood on acreage, but insists 'White Cliffs is more home to me now'.

'Another thing I became interested in was motorbikes. I learnt to ride when I was twenty-one. My brother Bluey put me on a bike and away I went around the bush tracks behind Lorne. I took a Honda 400 to Tasmania for a holiday but had an accident. I was OK, but my bike was "injured". It was then I joined the Motorbike Riders Association (MRA) Bendigo and my first trip was the Winton Bike Rally. That was the start of many motorbike rallies and camping trips from 1986 right up to 2002. I had a Yamaha 550, but in 1987 I bought a Harley-Davidson 883 Sportstar (1986), which I still have and ride. It's in the garage down south but will be coming up here eventually.

'My car is in a garage in town here, and around here I drive a Land Rover ute – the Urban Assault Vehicle – which I got for $500 off the estate of my brother's good mate Ron, who died last year. It was out of rego, so I got a permit, shoved all numerous layers of winter gear on and drove it up here, freezing all the way. The cops pulled me up to check it over and I must have looked like a terrorist, all covered up with layers, etc. Anyway, they were OK.

'I will get back on the Harley-Davidson. It is not so much the pain in my knee, but I'm a bit worried if I fell on it. I hope to bring the Harley up here soon, though.

'Anyway, in 1999 I took long service; then in 2000 I worked at Airport Strathdale Pre-School, and in 2001 I went to China for a while. By 2003 I knew I'd have to have the knee operation, so I finally took leave to have it done at the end of the year, and in 2004 went off to Ireland before coming to White Cliffs as part of the long recovery and sabbatical in early 2005.

'I first came here in 1975 when my parents were building the place. In fact, Matthew, my son, learnt to walk here. Later we brought motorbikes up here – the kids' as well as mine – and we always had fun here. Matthew at age seven learnt how to drive a ute as his grandfather would pay him to go off in the ute and bring back rocks to build into the walls. We've been coming here on and off all the time for thirty years. I still go noodling for opal. Don't do much underground work now. Either I do the maintenance work around the place, or Bluey does when he gets up here now and then.'

'A couple of tunes' – Ma plays Leila (left) and Wolfie (right) a bit of bluegrass.

At last, Ma emerges and we go into another room, where guitars lie around. This is her music room, where she and her friends play.

'Music has always been a big part of my life too. I majored in it at college – guitar and keyboards, now mainly banjo and guitar. I'm still trying to learn the Irish drum. I can also play the recorder and mouth organ. I was given an antique autoharp, which I'm still tuning.'

When you walk through the tunnels and rooms of the large underground dugout there are guitars and other musical instruments just lying around, but most are in the music room. Her brother Bluey is also a bit of a guitar player and a good country singer, as is his friend Lorraine.

Ma plays me a couple of tunes on a banjo and then on a rare resonator banjo that her brother picked up in Scotland. Ma mainly plays now in jam sessions and the occasional local event, but she played a lot in Bluey's band and on his CD. She just loves to play for the personal satisfaction. 'The locals have recently told me four of the local kids got guitars for Christmas and hinted at lessons,' she adds. 'I've already got an elderly chap and lady who want guitar lessons.'

I ask her what her favourite music is. 'Bluegrass music and more bluegrass music.' She also says she is now 'developing an interest in Willie Nelson and The Highwaymen'. She wins me with that. I love both. Bluegrass is 'happy' music to me on long trips.

Finally, I want to know what drives a woman with talent and qualifications to come to this remote, dusty part of western New South Wales. What is it about this place for her?

'Well, my grandfather Victor Dow was born in Broken Hill and became a station worker on Billila Station, on the Darling River near Wilcannia, where his parents were rouseabout and cook. Mum grew up there. It's not far from here. So I feel very much a bushie,

'My spirit place' – Ma Baker at Eagle's Nest on Turleys Hill.

my dad spent many years coming here and worked in the outback for years before he met Mum. White Cliffs is a unified community. Lots of friendship. I feel a part of it. I grew up on a small farmlet with a few cattle etc., and I still own a house that "runs scrub and rocks". I lived in town for five years and hated it. My place down south is out of town with a dam and such. My dogs used to swim in the dam all the time. Wolfie is a thirteen-year-old German Shepherd and Leila's a four-year-old beagle. Both beautiful, friendly mates.'

So here they are, the three of them, underground in a successful opal mine, with an art gallery of her father's paintings and pottery work – a cool, music retreat from the hot, dusty world outside, high on a hill with two cement eagles looking down. Bluey made them, as in the early days three live eagles used to perch on a pole and look down, so it became known as Eagle's Nest.

As the sun sets over the hill, a slight dust haze hangs in the air. It's still hot, but soon I hope it will be cooler as I head back south towards Wilcannia and onwards.

So how does Margaret Anne 'Ma' Baker sum up her life here in the outback in one sentence?

'It's my spirit place.'

(Since visiting Ma, there's been a few changes. She now works part-time both as an administrative clerk for National Parks and as an arts and music teacher for the Mission School in Wilcannia. She adds: 'My new partner Mal the miner and I have bought the dugout two doors down. And I can terrorise the locals on my Harley-Davidson – someone has to do it!')

I go outside to check out the heat. It is very slowly, very slowly dissipating, but it's still up around 40°C. All day has been spent trying to sleep and avoid the heat of near 50°C. Ma is back inside again, asleep somewhere underground in one of the many rooms. I return inside to crash onto the lounge-room couch, where the two dogs are also enjoying the dark and quietness and coolness.

I lie there thinking of last night's street party. The heat of the night was stifling, sitting outside in the street near the pub, and even numerous beers did little to enthuse me. I had hoped for a great outback evening. Ah well, just another experience ... You've got to have all sorts to make life interesting.

It is time to travel into the oncoming evening. I bid Ma farewell and leave her to her dogs and life underground. But before we leave White Cliffs, I stop to have a look at the huge solar panels that make up the town's electricity system. Why Australia doesn't totally embrace this technology is beyond me. We are a hot, dry country. We have huge open spaces and the panels take up miles less space than the hideous wind turbines that dot the landscape like a white plague. Costs would come down if solar was used by everyone, business and private. Something tells me governments won't make enough money out of it, so we as a society are stuck with fights over nuclear power, fossil fuels like coal, and wind turbines, which make some people wealthy. I know one man who has eighty-plus wind turbines on his various properties and he gets $7000 every year for each and every one of them. It is time we embraced technology that is good for the environment and the people of the planet. I like solar energy. I had solar panels on my home as far back as the early '80s when many people didn't have it, and my caravan was solar powered. My electric front gates at home are solar powered. Don't get me started on solar – I have a soapbox handy, so it's time to move on.

I am lost in deep thought about solar panels, Pro Hart and the trip ahead. Soon the dust rises in a solitary plume behind my ute as White Cliffs becomes smaller in the rear-view mirror.

I will soon again hit the intersection of the Cobb and Barrier highways. Now we head east towards Sydney.

Bang!

Before I leave the dirt I have a broken window to repair. A large stone has flung up out of nowhere. Such is life on the rough roads of the outback. I camp overnight beneath a few trees and enjoy the cool breeze and silence. Next morning, I hunt around on a nearby station and a small sheet of five-ply is cut to suit, taped and siliconed into place; it will suffice until the glass is replaced. Station people are great people. Don't abuse their generosity, though. Pay or at least offer to pay.

I had intended to go along the dirt road beside the Darling River to Tilpa and beyond, but I've lost time, and don't want dust getting in behind the temporary window. I head south and finally drive onto the bitumen of the Barrier Highway. We are heading east. After a drive reflecting on life and looking at the country, I finally pull into Cobar, 370 kilometres from White Cliffs via Wilcannia.

COBAR

At the crossroads of the Barrier Highway and Kidman Way, historic Cobar and the Cobar Shire covers a vast 44,065 square kilometres and is home to about 7000 people. A prosperous town blessed with a rich mining and pastoral heritage, there's a lot of history to explore here. It all started in 1870 when three tank sinkers and two Aboriginal guides were travelling from Bourke to

'Pastoral heritage' – artefacts on display from the pioneers who built Cobar.

'Rich mining heritage' – the Heritage Museum's old copper mine re-creation.

'The town's history' – the mighty Moreton Bay fig trees of Cobar.

Condobolin. Camped at Kubbur waterhole, near Cobar, they noticed the unusual colour of the water. The men took ore samples from the area and showed them to the publicans at the Gilgunnia Pub, a Mr and Mrs Kruge. Mrs Kruge had worked sorting ore in copper mines in Cornwall, England. She identified them as copper ore. The discovery led to the formation of the Great Cobar Copper Mine, which became the largest copper mine in Australia. At its peak in 1912, the Great Cobar boasted fourteen smelters, a 64-metre chimney stack and a workforce of over 2000. By around 1900, the population of Cobar was about 10,000.

One of the mines – the Cornish, Scottish & Australian (CSA) copper mine – had many openings and closures from the early 1870s on. In 1920 a fire broke out underground and burned for sixteen years. Cobar is still a mining town. Opposite the Heritage Centre a large statue of a hard-rock miner pays tribute to all miners who have lost their lives in Cobar mines.

Great bunch of trees in Cobar. Moreton Bay figs, in fact. When I arrive in town, I'm so impressed by them that I go in search of some further details. A lady in the supermarket suggests I talk to a lady up at the Heritage Centre. Someone in the café suggests the same lady. There's always one person in most bush towns who is the unofficial historian – the one who knows just about everything about anyone or anything in the entire history of the place since settlement. Sure enough, when I arrive at the centre I'm referred to a lady of mature years – the one who knows it all.

Yes, the Moreton Bay figs were planted by her grandfather, Sam Eves. And yes, she'll get onto the computer and find some more information for me. I leave her alone in her office and wander through the grand old two-storey building to look at the marvellous collections. Within half an hour I am ready to leave, and sure enough some printed material is given to me to read at my leisure. Such an obliging lady. Off I go, happier that I know a bit more about the Moreton Bay figs of Cobar and the town's history. The fig tree next to the post office is something that you should all go and see – how I'd love to have that growing outside my place.

GIDGIEGALAMBO STATION

'On this next trip I think I'll go to Gidgiegalambo,' I said.

'Where?' asked the wife.

'Gidgiegalambo, northwest of Cobar.'

'Why?'

'I like the name.'

'You like the name!'

And that's how I now come to end up at Gidgiegalambo.

'Yeah, and it's changed its name on various maps – I want to know why and what's there. Is it a sheep or cattle station, is it abandoned or is it still a working place?' I said, pointing to the tiny black dot on the map, as she looked over my shoulder before returning to the sink.

'You would.'

Patient woman, my wife Janette. She is used to me poring over maps and heading off into the wild blue yonder on a whim. She is used to me being a writer who has to go exploring. Nowadays, I feel sorry for some authors who never leave their tiny office and write books by looking at the internet. You don't know what a place is like by looking at a screen; you need to be on the spot to take in all senses of a place – the smells, the noises, the sights and often the tastes. You need to get a place deep into your soul to know what makes it tick.

'Give a man a map and he has a library,' the writer Mary Gilmore once said. I'm always intrigued by what you find on maps. I have hundreds of them and it never ceases to amaze me what you find.

I saw Gidgiegalambo on a map and just liked the name. It was an outback western New South Wales station, just a tiny dot on a map. Months later on another map I saw it spelt 'Gidgie'. Then I lost the piece of paper I wrote the name on with directions, and I couldn't remember where it was on the map. All I remembered was that it was in New South Wales.

Many months later, I found the name again, and then I saw it wasn't on the latest map in my collection. Why? Has it disappeared, did someone decide to reduce its name and then remove it from all maps? Well, me being me, an inquisitive bastard, I wasn't going to let it go by.

'So when do you leave?' asked Janette.

'There's some rocky ground around here' – Allan and one of Gidgie's small stones!

'No one home' – bush wisdom: 'Shut the gate, mate!' Duly noted.

'I've got some other places and interviews I need to do, so I'll include it in the trip.'

'Want your jeans ironed?'

Women are so clear on what the priorities are. Me, I'm happy just to chuck some stuff in the back of the ute and be off. Not my wife. She is a wonder woman.

For me, it's about 700 kilometres from home, but only 105 kilometres from Cobar, so I have to see it and I'm not going to rest until I put this story to bed. I leave Cobar and head back to the dirt roads once more. Gidgiegalambo here I come!

Ah well – you can't win all the time.

No one is available to talk about Gidgie with me. But at least I have been there now. There is no mailbox or sign on the property gate; the only sign is a shire one that says it's a no through road. They don't tell you that the further you drive down the road the worse it becomes or when you go up over the rocky ranges it gets even rougher. Creek beds wash away, by the looks of the area, even though it is now in drought.

There's no one home, only the numerous kelpie dogs. You should never go wandering around people's station sheds or homestead yards without permission, so I bid the dogs farewell and made my way back along the rough track to rejoin the road north. One thing's for sure: there's some rocky ground around here, huge slabs of rock in fact.

There's no signs that mention Gidgie, Gidgee or Gidgiegalambo anywhere. Gidgie is in gidgee country. What is gidgee? Gidgee refers to a number of closely related species of acacia, or wattles as they are commonly known. There's a few: *Acacia anastema*, commonly known as sandridge gidgee or just gidgee; *Acacia pruinocarpa*, commonly known as gidgee or black gidgee; and *Acacia subtessaroqona*, commonly known as spreading gidgee.

From Gidgie it is easy to locate where I am on the map. I have plenty of names to lead me in the right direction, including some great Aussie place names like Cuttygullyaroo Tank to the nor-west, Titagoonah to the nor-east, Curranyalpah to the sou-east and Kerrigundi Tank to the west. How could you get lost with that lot? Don't you just want to visit them all, just to see why they have these great names? No? Well I do, 'cause I love Australia and want to see everything.

Onwards I go towards the Darling River, pleased I've made the effort to see somewhere off the beaten path. Soon afterwards, I see a sign that adds to the mystery and brings me to a screaming halt: 'Gambolalley'. A sign on two gates on opposite sides of the road.

When I made some enquiries prior to my trip, I was told that a previous owner of Gidgie also had a property called Galambo and he had added it to Gidgie to come up with Gidgiegalambo. That's one story; another is that Galambo is a creek, but I can't find it on the map.

Did someone misspell an original word? Should it really read Gidgiegambo? Or Gidgiegambolalley? I love a mystery. All because I found different spellings on maps, and it has led me to this.

Interesting country – and I still like the name Gidgiegalambo.

(PS. I've solved the mystery! More recently, I hired a Cessna to fly over the Murray River. In the office at the airport was a huge aeronautical map – and there it was, a few kilometres from the homestead – Gidgiegalambo Creek! Now I want to find out what the name means. It is the only map I've seen with the creek listed on it. I love being a detective solving things!)

LOUTH

I arrive at Louth, on the Darling, for a break at Shindy's Inn and a yarn with a semi-local bloke. He comes from Sydney each year for three months at a time to chase fish. Even when there's none, he still comes. He loves the life in this tiny place.

We talk about the town 'treasure'. Supposedly, the headstone of Mary Mathews (wife of Thomas Andrew Mathews, the town's founder) is positioned in the local cemetery so that it catches the light of the setting sun and reflects it through town. On her birthday, 19 August, the reflected light lands on the front door of the house in Louth in which she lived.

Well, I can't vouch for that – it wasn't 19 August – but I did find the large memorial to Mary in the cemetery, near the pub.

In 1888 Dunlop Station, south of the town, became the first sheep station in the world to use mechanical shears. It was a such a revolution in sheep shearing that the Governor of New South Wales visited the shed to see it for himself.

Left: 'The town treasure' – the Mary Mathews memorial in Louth cemetery.

Below: 'Cattle and sheep don't mix with aircrafts' – more bush wisdom.

TOORALE STATION

West of Bourke, Toorale can claim to have had Henry Lawson working there in 1892. Lawson wrote about it later. He had walked to Toorale to work as a rouseabout. The 46-stand shed where he laboured for a month lugging fleeces is now abandoned. In Lawson's time, Toorale – wedged between the Warrego and Darling rivers – was part of one of the greatest pastoral empires New South Wales has ever known and its shed sheared more than 250,000 sheep a year.

Next stop is Bourke, 67 kilometres to the northeast.

'Private property' – signs of every description everywhere.

IT'S HOT – BLOODY HOT!

I spend time just wandering along under some trees, having a break from driving. The oppressive heat saps the energy, but I sip on a water bottle. I often wear a wet handkerchief around the throat to keep sweat from running down my back when out here. People usually only travel and see the outback in the cooler winter months, but by doing so they never really get to feel the outback as it would have been when Burke and Wills died of thirst, or to feel what it would have been like to have been an early settler going into unknown lands and trying to survive. I'm not, however, saying you all should go out there in the middle of summer. I have a very deep respect for the explorers and pioneer settlers of Australia. Every time I head outback I am amazed at how the early settlers survived this land. They were a truly great people. We can drive a section today in a few hours in air-conditioned comfort, drinking cool water and eating as we go. They, on the other hand, would take many weeks to travel the same distance, cooking their meagre supplies or searching for water and wild food to shoot – and do it all in near 50°C heat, covered in flies.

We have it so easy today, but it is nice to feel something of what it was like for them. As a writer I like to put myself right into those early settlers' shoes and experience it. Mind you, I only get a small sample of it, before again retreating to the air-conditioner, like everyone else. Travelling on foot in this country just with a canvas water-bag and no shade is something I don't really want to experience to any lengthy degree.

Recently, I spent a week in Broken Hill when it was over 40°C each day, and when I drove less than 100 kilometres away, it was 49°C. Be prepared for extremes in the outback. Heat will sap your energy during the day, and by night the temperature could drop below zero.

Flies are a curse in the outback. Next time you're being swarmed by thousands of the little blighters in the hot dry bush just remember the following: there are 120,000 types of flies, they vomit on food instantly on landing, they live for an average of twenty-one days, their wings beat at 200 times a second, they don't grow (they are born full size), they jump backwards when taking off and fly at an average a speed of 8 km/h; they smell with their antenna, they will beat their wings only if their feet are free, their wings are attached to their eyes internally, they have 4000 lens in each eye, and they go to sleep almost immediately at 4°C.

BOURKE

How many times have we heard people say, 'It's the back o' Bourke' or 'I've been to the back o' Bourke and back', referring to some long trip they've been on? Most have never actually been to Bourke, New South Wales. The now famous expression was first coined by Scottish-born poet Will Ogilvie and became part of our

'The real outback' – entering historic Bourke.

national lingo way back in the days when a trip to Bourke was a real effort – on a long, hot, dry track or on paddleboats that often got stuck and stranded for months. In the days of early shearers and swagmen, Bourke was a long way outback. Now it's a normal drive, although it can be a hot and lonely one, especially if you follow the Darling River on dusty or boggy roads. There's no in-between – it's either dusty or boggy, depending on the weather.

Bourke is changing, and not for the better. Graffiti and vandalism are common, whereas when I was here in 2000 there was next to none. The café where I enjoyed a break is now closed and covered with security mesh, its windows broken. Other shops near it are in the same condition. I'm told one shopowner refuses to reinstall windows, but he keeps his shop open and relies on mesh only to keep intruders at bay. It looks terrible. A feeling of growing desperation is present. While taking some photos of the Henry Lawson memorial in a park, I am dismayed to discover that some of the other memorials have been destroyed or covered in graffiti since I was last here.

'Part of our national lingo' – memorial to poet Will Ogilvie.

'Smile' – they like to keep an eye on things out here.

One of the local attractions is the Back o' Bourke Museum. It will be good when it's finished because it will give travellers an insight into the history of this town on the Darling and its surrounds. Stage 2 work is commencing the day after I leave. I've tried to visit it a few times; once it was closed, the second time the theatrette was closed, and today the whole place is closed. I wait for half an hour until finally a man appears from out the back and tells me he'll ring to see why it isn't open. Shortly afterwards another man arrives to open it for me – the lady is running late for work. About fifteen minutes later, the show in the theatrette is finished and I am thanked for coming. Needless to say, I'm pretty unimpressed. I have stayed in town overnight and delayed leaving until I got to see it. But I will return when the museum's completed; if the slide show is any indication, it will be worth seeing.

HENRY LAWSON'S TREK TO THE BORDER

Well, we are going back o' Bourke and then further out. From Bourke, we start to head northwest towards the Queensland border town of Hungerford. The route is the same as the one that Henry Lawson walked and wrote about in 1892.

For me, it is a great chance to see the land my hero visited. I have travelled many kilometres on many occasions and to many locations to see a place visited by Henry Lawson. Obviously, lots of things have changed after 100 years, but you can still get a feeling for what he experienced.

The book *A Stranger on the Darling*, written by the late Alan Barton and his daughter Robyn Burrows, was published a few years ago. It tells of Henry's time on the Darling.

'The lady behind the bar' – Andrea Rudd.

FORDS BRIDGE TO TIBOOBURRA

ANDREA RUDD, WARREGO WOMAN

'I'm a boots 'n' all type of person. I come up with an idea and go for it. My family just shake their heads.'

Fords Bridge, New South Wales. Population: 3.

As I pull up outside the Warrego Hotel in this tiny place 70 kilometres northwest of Bourke, I'm met by a black-and-tan red healer–kelpie cross, who comes over to have a sniff while accepting pats and a g'day. I don't notice at the time that he has no tail.

Cheery greetings inside the pub – one from a bloke at the bar in a white Akubra and one from the lady behind the bar. A couple

'Northwest of Bourke' – Warrego River bridge.

of light stubbies and a yak and the bloke is off. He's just driven from Tamworth and still has a three-hour drive to help a mate doing mustering on a station property up the track. Andrea, the lady behind the bar, settles in for a yarn. I gather that she's an interesting woman. Can I interview her? Yeah, why not.

Born on the Queensland Sunshine Coast in 1964, Andrea is the daughter of Brian Rudd, who pioneered the teaching of babies as young as eight weeks to swim. Her mother was also a swimming teacher. Her parents divorced when she was ten. Andrea's older brother Paul is a builder in Beaudesert. Growing up was spent half in Brisbane and half at Mooloolaba. When she left school, Andrea first did office work, but soon found out she didn't belong behind a desk, so she became a swimming teacher too and learnt all the tricks of the trade for four or five years from her father in his business at Acacia Ridge.

Before then, she had learnt to skydive, when just sixteen.

'I learnt by default. I was helping a mate do stocktaking in his motorbike shop. He was a skydiver himself so instead of paying me he said, "I'll give you your first skydive as payment." So away I went, and ended up skydiving for the next twenty years as a sport and I also became an instructor. I have done a total of about 1000 jumps. In 1986, when I was twenty-two, I went overseas on a skydiving holiday to Europe. It was at a competition in Norway, north of Oslo, that I met Paul. He was a Norwegian and two weeks later we married for convenience. I could stay there and it would make it easier for him to come to Australia. We lived in Norway, and I just did waitress jobs or whatever until we came back to Australia in 1988.

'Immediately we signed up to compete in the Ayers Rock to the Gold Coast camel race. For the next three-and-a-half months, it was each rider with one camel across Australia. It was decided to put Paul on the camel and I was Paul's back-up. He became a bit of a star in the documentary as the Norwegian who fell off his

'Population: 3' – Fords Bridge, New South Wales.

camel nearly every day. It was such an amazing time. It was, however, too rushed – a bit cruel on the camels – but the trip was just a terribly life-changing experience.

'During the trip, we met Chris and Kristie Ware-Smiles and later they invited us to visit them at Mudgee for a while. We ended up staying there for two years! We went and caught wild camels on the edge of the Simpson Desert and walked them back along the Oodnadatta Track to Macumber Station, and then trucked them home to Mudgee, where we started to build wagons. A couple of interludes around that time included us all appearing at Darling Harbour in Sydney doing the three-wise-men-and-camels thing, and we also did the Bundaberg Rum Camel Race Team at the Sydney Show.'

By 1990 the two couples were ready, and with Paul and Andrea in one wagon and Chris and Kristie in another they left for a big trip.

'Chris and Kristie also took their kids – two girls, six and ten, and a two-month-old baby. Travelling from Wollar, near Mudgee, we headed west to Bourke, Wanaaring, Tibooburra, through the Corner Country, but there Chris and Kristie decided to head for home. Paul and I carried on down the Strzelecki Track to Lyndhurst, then took the Marree track to Anna Creek Station (where we left the camels). We hitched a ride into Pitjantjatjara country to Fregon. We knew one of the elders there as he was on our team when we raced the camels across Australia. We caught some wild camels there and walked them to Marla Bore, then trucked them to Oodnadatta and walked them to Anna Creek.

'From there we walked to Marree and then up the Birdsville Track. We were behind schedule and would have missed getting to the Birdsville races in time, so we hitched a ride up to

Birdsville to meet up with old friends, both skydivers and camel people. Going back to Munnerangie, where we'd left the camels, we had an accident. The car came over a sandy rise and at the bottom was a huge hole filled with bull-dust. The car dug in and crashed. I was in the back seat and had my front teeth wiped out – three days later I finally managed to beg a ride on the mail plane and then had two weeks of dental torture in Port Augusta. I managed to beg my way onto the mail plane again and returned to Birdsville. It had been a bad time; we'd also just lost our dog Buddy, who at the end of a hot day accidentally jumped into a boiling-hot water bore. He was such a good dog.

'At Birdsville we had a camel give birth to a calf, so it travelled in the wagon in a sling on the seat. From Birdsville the camel wagon headed east to Bettota, then down south to Innamincka, Burke and Wills Dig Tree on the Cooper, and Santos and Tibooburra.

'Before we got there, though, the mother of the calf went lame, so we got her and the calf into the mail truck – out here they carry anything. We had to tie all the mail bags onto the outside of the truck so our camel had room. She was sent to Tibooburra to recover and we planned to collect her later, which we did.

'Eventually we ended up 40 kilometres west of Wanaaring at Urisino Station – a fabulous old homestead of mud-brick which no one was living in. Abandoned. Originally the station was 1 million acres. We did a deal with the owners that we would renovate the homestead in return for a lease. For the next eight years we ran it as a guesthouse and gave camel rides as well. It had an airstrip and we had a lot of high-flyers come out to stay – people like Dick Smith and the Lowy family [owners of Westfield shopping centres].

'Then the wheels fell off it all – the owners of the property wanted to sell up. We left the same way we arrived, by camel wagon. We had two wagons and a sulky and a bunch of camels. We walked them to a station in the Fords Bridge area.'

Among all this activity Paul and Andrea still found time to travel back to Norway four or five times.

'About 1995 on one trip we left near 50° outback heat to arrive in Norway, where it was minus 30°C. I ended up with indigenous Laplanders way up north, and for three weeks lived with them as we went on a reindeer muster. It was mid-winter, so the sun never gets above the horizon – it's just a few hours of twilight, then it goes into darkness. I had about thirty layers of clothing and was freezing. The Lappish women took me to a hut and re-dressed me. Just one layer underneath and then total reindeer skins for clothing. No socks, just dry grass in the boots. I was so warm. We mustered thousands of reindeers on snow scooters, and you tie them onto sleds towed by reindeer and travel about 200 kilometres back, and then they were drafted out as each had ear tags for identification. It

Near 50° outback heat – vapour trail in the sky.

'Born without a tail' – Andrea and Bare Arse outside the pub.

was nothing but reindeer for food – reindeer soup, reindeer stew and nothing else. It was an amazing experience.'

As usual, life for Andrea was never dull. She made another decision.

She moved to Noosa to run a swimming school in August 1998. She took over her father's business so that he could retire. Between 1998 and 2006 she was a lifesaver at Noosa Heads Surf Lifesaving Club and competed in numerous surf carnivals. In 2000 Paul returned to Norway to live.

Another life change happened in March 2006, when she again headed west to become the new owner of the Warrego Hotel at Fords Bridge.

'When I bought the pub it was a "1913 renovator's delight": another mud-brick building, filthy, lime green inside and out, bare concrete floors, no trees, garden. It had closed two years before. When I opened I had various nutcases help me out. Now here I am. I did some swimming teaching in Bourke as well – local kids, and some babies. That's what I am best at, teaching babies to survive in water. I've taught eighteen-month-old kids to swim the length of the pool; they learn how to roll over and float to have a rest.'

Bare Arse the dog comes into the pub for a pat and a hello. He got his name due to the fact that he was born without a tail. Andrea found him advertised for sale as a four-month-old-pup, on the internet. 'He's king of the kids during the day. He loves kids, but when I close up he becomes the full-on guard dog. No one would get in here after dark.'

Life changes often happen for Andrea. She adapts.

'I'll see how I go here, will stay for as long as I want, but being tied to a pub seven days a week can be tiring. I hope to find someone to assist. I'm not afraid to have a go at anything. I've worked as a barmaid, done office work, cooking and cleaning, mustering, catering (as a camp oven cook), been a car washer, book-keeper, gardener, swim teacher, skydiving instructor, camel trainer, renovator … Hmm, what else have I done?

'I still have so many things I'd like to do one day – like go play with elephants in Africa. I still want to do a lot more travel, including South America. I love the beach and the outback about fifty–fifty. I love the red sand people, but I go back and forth to the waves. I'm a boots 'n' all type of person. I come up with an idea and go for it. My family just shake their heads.'

Andrea and I discuss many aspects of travel and the places we've both been to, and what cranks our engine in the great outdoors. We share similar ideas of what is good about travel.

She really is a mad camel lover. For her the best thing about slow travel by camel is 'seeing every sunrise and sunset in the outback, meeting people, and at the pace you travel you see everything. I had a great relationship with my camels and my chooks.'

And what is the negative side?

'Probably people asking the same dumb questions all the time and being rude with cameras. Now, too, adventures seem harder due to insurance claims – you have to be a lot more careful.'

So what else is Andrea looking for out of life?

'I'm looking for a 6-foot 2-inch man – who likes camels,' she laughs as she finishes rolling another fag.

I doubt that life will ever be dull for this active, independent and resourceful lady.

THE BORDER: CLOSE THE BLOODY GATE!

Hungerford – population: 11, just over the border in Queensland – is 150 kilometres northwest of Fords Bridge.

'They take closing the gate seriously up here' – Dog Fence gate.

It is the only town I've been to where you have to open the gate to get in. In doing so, you're crossing the border from New South Wales into Queensland. The gate is in the dingo (or dog) fence right on the edge of town. Go 100 metres from the gate and you are at the pub. Opening this gate was something that really thrilled me. It is always good to have a memorable experience in a town. I've told many people since about the town with the gate. No one knew about it until I told them. And they take closing the gate seriously up here. A sign here says that if you don't close it, a penalty not exceeding $1000 applies.

I book a bed for the night at the Royal Mail Hotel. I move my ute alongside the long verandah and enter my room with my gear. The doors all lead off the front verandah. I return to the bar and order a beer. Now, you can usually find someone to write about if you sit in a pub, and on this trip, this is the pub. This one I will write about in some detail, just to show some of the people you meet on

'An interesting place with some characters' – the Royal Mail Hotel.

'She certainly doesn't look her age' – the main bar.

the road. Something tells me the Royal Mail is an interesting place with some characters. It doesn't take long to find out.

Jim orders his first drinks at the bar. He's just finished work. A Carlton beer, a double vodka and a Stones green ginger. Soon all three are sitting beside each other on the bar. I want to see if he actually drinks them. Sure enough, they disappear. Handbag, his lovely dog, sits patiently at the front door, looking in. Jim says he thinks she is pregnant to the only dog capable in town. The male dug his way under the fence and made her acquaintance.

Peter Young and his better half Rhelma Quinlivan own this great outback pub. Chubby Cheeks, their little Jack Russell, is darting to and fro and playing with Handbag. Peter spent forty years at sea 'chasing prawns and other water life' until he lost his boat due to a fire off Ballina. Peter and Rhelma were in South Australia on holiday, trying to decide what to do, when they heard John Laws mention on his radio show that the pub at Hungerford was up for sale. They immediately decided to go have a look. They bought it on the spot. A major change of lifestyle for a man of the sea. They left their homes and family in Ballina and have now been at the Royal Mail for seven years, but now it is time to move on. Rhelma says she will retire at seventy, in a couple of years, or else! She certainly doesn't look her age.

Ian sits in the corner and he and I get to talking. He is a fencer from Swan Hill, northern Victoria, but born in cold Kyneton in central Victoria. He's a long way from home. He is working with a fencing contractor about 100 kilometres southwest of here and will return to work in a couple of days. 'We still have 250 kilometres of fencing to finish on this job,' he says matter-of-factly. I say he'd be used to the heat, surely, coming from Swan Hill. He tells me that the first day he arrived to start work out west was in February; a gauge was placed on the ground next to the post he was installing and it read 57°C in the sun. There was no shade anywhere. 'I didn't think I'd ever get to see it that hot. You get used to it – eventually.'

Two young plumbers arrive from work. They've been working in the national park just north of here. When one of them learns I'm a writer, he says I must go to Eulo, up the track, to the date farm. He gives it a good rap. Sure enough, his parents, Ian and Nan Pike, own it. I note down the details. I'll get there one day, but not on this trip. I am keen to try the hot artesian mud pools; the plumber is keen to tell me about. I also want to go further north from here to see the bilby project within the national park. Sadly, though, time is against me – I have a man to see in Tibooburra. (Had I known at the time I would end up missing him, I could have gone on north. I don't always arrange interviews ahead, as outback travel can often lead me on side trips.)

Soon I will get to meet a Hungerford legend – Mac. His photo is on the pub wall, where he's driving his Model T ute. There's memorabilia all around: on the walls, outside on the verandah and around the yards. Rhelma says the pub had been stripped when they arrived, so she set to and collected more and more from a wide area. It looks great. We talk long about history and especially about that great Aussie writer who drank in the bar here and wrote about Hungerford – Henry Lawson, my hero and 'the first articulate voice of Australia', as one biographer many years ago so rightly described him. I promise to send her a heap of photos and information on Henry to add to those on the walls, as soon as I get home. Above the bar is a large framed photo of a nude woman. She is Hungerford Chloe. Mac found it in his shed and asked if Rhelma wanted it for the pub – or was it too risqué? Rhelma loved it and soon had it framed and installed. You have to see Hungerford Chloe.

A tall, lanky man in an old hat wanders in while I am having my steak and vegies in the dining room. I know who he is. He looks a legend.

I am introduced to Mac as I order a beer. We yarn together for quite a while. He came to Hungerford to work on a property in 1951, and has since done other work – stockman on horseback, station manager, road construction contractor and such. He did well for himself. He'll never leave. Max is eighty, drives a Model T ute, but is 'a Toyota man'. He owns two Land Cruiser utes and a new Land Cruiser wagon. Mac's a nice bloke. Easy to like.

Soon it is time for me to retire; it's been a long day. I wander off to room number 3 along the verandah, and relax in the large room – pine panelled and corrugated-iron walls. I have the choice of a double bed or two singles. A table, chairs and fridge make up the rest of the room, with an air-conditioner in the wall. Very clean and comfortable; no TV to waste time with. I relax with a

'A Toyota man' – Mac and his T-model Ford.

'Mac can fix anything' – Mac and grader.

hot cuppa and write some notes. Rhelma gave me a heap of notes concerning the history of the pub and the town, and some clippings about Henry Lawson. The only noise is the air-conditioner and the occasional laugh from people seated beneath the verandah. The two dogs enjoy being part of the small group.

This place reeks of history. If only I could go back and share an ale with Henry Lawson in the same bar all those years ago. I am relaxed and at peace with the world.

Later on, I walk back from the shower block out in the backyard. The night is dark, and I look up to see my old friends, the stars of the Southern Cross. I always feel comfortable when I can see them in any night sky. But more so when travelling alone in the outback, and even more so when there's no mobile phone reception like tonight and I can't have my nightly conversation with Janette at home. It is on these nights that she, too, looks up at the Southern Cross, knowing I'm out there and thinking of her.

Next morning, bright and early, I have breakfast while talking with Rhelma. It's now 9 am, so I go see Mac. Now, Mac will have his full story written, but not today. Shortly, I have to head off south and east to the next part of the trip. But I do have to call in for a yarn again.

Mac shows me his collection: road graders, front-end loaders, bulldozer, trucks, caravan, boat, bus and more. Locals tell me Mac can fix anything and usually does; he's called on by all to assist wherever, whenever. He is good friends with Peter and Rhelma and helps out with their mail run when needed, and he and Peter work closely together. 'I made the mistake of getting married late in life,' Mac says. But she's gone and he's happy to spend the rest of his days in Hungerford. Mac says his nephew, who is into heavy equipment too, will get the Model T ute and boat; and, I assume, he will probably end up with all of Mac's collection. We wander and yarn among his possessions. The little grey Fergie tractor is his current project – it should be fixed by late afternoon. I reckon Jim's nephew is going to have a lot of fun with 'projects', just like Mac. 'He's a collector too,' says Mac.

Far too soon, I have to leave. I could spend a day with this friendly, gentle man. 'I'll be back for another yarn,' I tell him. 'Better not leave it too long,' he says with a laugh. He's had some health problems and operations, but he stills looks fit and reminds me of Chips Rafferty – tall, lanky and weather-worn, with a bush hat to match.

And so I head south again, careful to make sure I close the gate. One last look and a photo, and it's time to go. Fancy having to open and close a gate to get into a town; I reckon that's hilarious, very Australian. Unlike border gates in other countries, there are no guards with machine-guns on our gates. It's a pity that morons seem to think they need to plaster stickers all over ours, though. Why would some idiot put a sticker on the fence gate at Hungerford to advertise a windscreen service in Sydney? Sometimes I just can't work out some people. Just like the idiots that write 'Mario loves Lucy' on a rock in the middle of nowhere. Graffiti junkies aren't artists, they are bloody vandals.

'No guards with machine-guns' – but please close the gate.

'Westwards for Wanaaring' – dust and stone.

A WORD ON THE LINGO

I turn off to head westwards for Wanaaring, lost in my thoughts of my brief but nice time in town. I knew I was in Queensland when a bloke in the pub kept saying 'eh'. If someone says 'eh' at the end of every sentence, you can be pretty sure you're talking to either a Northern Territorian or a Queenslander. If they refer to everything as 'down south', they're probably a Territorian or possibly a Queenslander. If it's someone sticking it up the Vics, they'll be a South Australian or a Western Australian, both of whom for some reason have a big hang-up on Vics. If they refer to Mexicans, it will be someone from New South Wales talking about Victorians. A croweater is a South Aussie, a banana bender a Queenslander, and a double-header a Tasmanian – or a Taswegian, as some call them. So what do they call Western Australians, NSWers, NTers and ACTers? Someone said the W in Western Australia stands for whinger, the A in ACT for arseholes (politician country) and, of course, NTers everyone knows as Territorians, although I reckon a good name would be stubbie wranglers.

You can often pick up small differences in lingo when you listen as you travel Australia. Now, I married a South Aussie and after thirty years of marriage I still haven't convinced her that trombone is really called pumpkin. I've brainwashed her to become a St Kilda supporter, but I detect there's still a hidden feeling for those mongrel Crows.

In New South Wales and Queensland it is a hard battle to show them that Aussie Rules is really the national sport, and they insist on playing those other minor games like rugby league and union. They can't even make up their mind which way to go. WA, SA and Tassie were easily converted many years ago; NT is a bit of both, but AFL does have a strong hold there.

Ah, Australia — land of diversity.

So now we head further into the rough country and follow the Dog Fence. But you can't go along it or next to it; the authorities reckon it is out of bounds, even though some people do use it. Sometimes you just have to believe you have permission until someone tells you otherwise. But no, I'll be good and stick to the roads to the south and then west. We will come back to the Dog Fence, though.

WANAARING

It's time for a break and a ham, cheese and tomato sanga with a cuppa in Wanaaring, 102 kilometres south and then west of Hungerford.

Four people on two motorbikes are the only other people in the roadhouse. I start chatting to one of the men, who with his mate and two women have been touring the outback on large off-road motorbikes. He informs me of the dirt road conditions ahead for Tibooburra and I do the same for him for Hungerford. That's where they are headed before going back towards the east coast to their home in Brisbane.

I am amazed when he brags about 'easily' doing 130 km/h on the dirt tracks and that 'the bikes are built for it' — sure, the bike can do it, but he is not only putting himself at risk but also his wife, on the back of the bike. Out here city people think that because there's little traffic and wide open country you can go berserk. What he hasn't taken into account are the hundreds of kangaroos, emus, wild goats, horses, cattle and sheep that wander the countryside and are always attracted to feeding alongside the roads and tracks. He has also ignored the fact that there are bull-dust hiding holes in the road that can spell disaster for cars and utes, let alone a motorbike – or maybe he just doesn't know about them. And to come around a blind corner could mean a head-on with a vehicle; or, if he rides into dust coming from another vehicle it would mean he'd be riding blind until well past the other vehicle. To be in such isolated country and have an accident at such a high speed is really courting injury, if not death.

The four bikers move outside to sit and eat their meal, and when I move outside to leave, one man notices that his front wheel has 'developed' a dent in the hub, thus explaining the 'slight vibration' through the steering wheel. A conversation between them ensues, the know-all expressing his confidence. So much for their high-speed holiday. I leave them to it. I bid them farewell – 'May the wind be at your backs and the road stays safe.'

You idiots!

Soon they are long behind me and I make way westwards. To Tibooburra, my destination for the day.

TIME OUT

I want to take some time out here, put the billy on and just relax. It's a nice spot, a slight breeze wafts through the few trees around. That whispering sound is the wind blowing through the native pines – the slightest breeze and these trees will 'talk' to you. At night, lying in a swag during that time between relaxing and drifting off into a deep sleep, it can be a soothing sound, a quiet breath-like whisper on the wind. Some may not agree with me and think it sounds like a ghost whispering, but I don't get that feeling; I find it relaxing.

Anyway, I'm sitting underneath these trees, out of the sun, waiting for the billy to boil, when I see something on the ground near me: an antlion hole. I thought you might like to know about this tiny creature that is worldwide in distribution, but most common in arid and sandy habitats. Many people don't know of it and, whenever I've shown them, they are always amazed by the little blighters. Being non-scientific, I can only explain them as having their kneecaps on back to front, so their movements appear to be the opposite to what we'd expect. Many campers may never be aware they are there, although some will notice their traps.

I want to illustrate just how interesting the natural world can be and that just because you're in hot, dry, sandy, dusty country, it doesn't mean there isn't life out here. There is, and this is just a tiny, tiny example. I want to tell you of it to show that you can take time out to relax and look and also learn at the same time.

The antlion is a tiny insect. The larva eats ants and other insects, while the fully grown adult antlion eats pollen and nectar. The larva is often called a doodlebug, because it leaves a winding, weaving track that looks like someone has doodled in the sand.

The antlion larva sets about digging a pit by crawling backwards, using its belly to shovel soil. It uses its front to put heaps of soil onto its head and with a sharp flick deposits the soil away from the area. It repeats its moves in circles and eventually the pit gets deep enough for the larva to settle down in the bottom, where it buries itself with only its jaws above the surface. Any small insects that venture or fall into the trap are seized upon and the fluids sucked from their bodies by the jaws of the larva. If an insect tries to escape, the antlion larva will flick showers of sand or dirt at the prey until it slips down into the trap and into its jaws. The average size of the trap is 50 centimetres deep and 75 centimetres wide at the edge.

From egg to adulthood may take up to three years. The adult antlion is mostly found in soft sand beneath trees or under overhanging rocks. It is a very feeble flyer and is normally found fluttering about in the night, in search of a mate. The adult is rarely seen in the wild because it is usually active only in the evening.

Well, that's just a brief look at one tiny insect out here in the outback. So keep an eye out on the ground for the tell-tale signs of their prey traps. Not all interesting wildlife is cute and cuddly or spectacular, but even little insects make up a vital part of the world around us. Another thing; you can impress the hell out of your kids when you show them stuff like this. They'll reckon their own 'outback dad' is just like Harry Butler, Steve Irwin and the Leyland Brothers all rolled into one.

The first time I showed people antlions was when I gave a talk to tourists at a national park. I did a night-time slide show. Not only were the kids fascinated by antlions, but adults couldn't believe it either. They were also impressed when I showed them how to tell what animals were in the area, just by looking at dried animal turds!

I head across the southeast edge of Sturt National Park – 325,000 hectares of tough land, but one of diversity and interest.

Imagine harsh, rugged, flat, open desert terrain in all directions. Add in the middle a huge pile of rocks. Rocks of all shapes and sizes – hectares after many hectares of them. These are 450-million-year-old red granite tors. Add just to the edge of all this a

'Heaps of rocks' – rocks millions of years old in Tibooburra.

small township. That's Tibooburra. It's one of the hottest and most isolated places in New South Wales. The rocky outcrops in and around town add a great interest to the region – Tibooburra is said to mean 'heaps of rocks' in the local Aboriginal language.

I could write a book about this country and the explorers like Sturt who roamed through here in the 1840s. I never cease to be amazed by our explorers and the country they developed under what must have been exceedingly stressful and exhausting conditions. That's another story for another book at some other time.

TIBOOBURRA

An excellent display of the history of the area can be found at the National Parks and Wildlife office in the main street of Tibooburra. The local Aboriginal Land Council also has a small but interesting exhibition of Aboriginal wood and stone artefacts from the Wadigali, Wongkumara and Malyangapa tribes at the Keeping Place, on the southern edge of town.

For me, though, all I want is a bed for the night and some tucker. I get the last bed in town by pure luck. The whole town is booked out by drilling teams maintaining the gas pipeline. I'm having a yarn and a cuppa with the shopkeeper when a truckie from down south comes to get a bed and is not too impressed he's missed out. I notice he has a sleeper-cab on his truck, so at least he has a bed for the night. I guess he's looking for a room with TV, shower and the other facilities. He leaves to sort out his own night ahead – he walks straight across the road to the pub.

I have a meal at the same pub later on, sitting under the verandah beneath some nice trees, watching people come and go as the sun slowly sets. Most of them are workmen, obviously pipeline workers, in four-wheel drives or trucks carrying heavy

'Isolated' – the sign for Tibooburra.

equipment. A few tourists in decked-out four-wheel drives arrive and have their meal inside the pub, but I prefer being outside beneath the trees.

Tibooburra is isolated – 335 kilometres north of Broken Hill, 1504 kilometres northwest of Sydney, 900 kilometres from Adelaide. It is just 183 metres above sea level. Explorer Charles Sturt and his party were the first white people in the area in 1845. Burke and Wills followed in 1860 on their ill-fated expedition north to the Gulf of Carpentaria. The tiny town was first known as The Granite or Granite Rush, when gold was discovered at Mt Browne and then at Tibooburra itself in 1881.

In the 1930s the entire original local Aboriginal population was moved to Brewarrina.

I return my empty plate and beer glass to the main bar and thank the landlady for the nice meal. The Family Hotel, built from local stone in 1883, is famous for the painted murals on most

'Search for the inland sea' – replica of Sturt's boat.

of the walls. Clifton Pugh, Russell Drysdale, Rick Amor and more recent works by Howard William Steer (who I'll be talking to a bit later on) add an unusual beauty to the place.

I walk across the road and enjoy the cool of the evening on the small verandah of my cabin. Night soon closes in and another day is done.

First thing in the morning I go to the edge of town to photograph the sculpture in Pioneer Park – a replica of the 27-foot-long whaleboat Charles Sturt carried across the country on a wagon while on his search for the inland sea. It is perched upside down on four poles.

I wish I had more time to explore the Sturt National Park, but I shall return yet again – it is a favourite place. I like nothing better than to stand on gibber plains that extend for as far as the eye can see in all directions. The park has a wide range of topography: clay-pans rising to red sandhills, dry creek beds with rocky gorges, and isolated 'jump-up' mesas rising up to 150 metres above the surrounding flatlands. Gibber plains (stony desert) are my favourite, though. The great dingo fence – the Dog Fence, which we first encountered south of Hungerford – forms a part of the Sturt park's boundary. It's the world's longest fence, stretching some 5000-plus kilometres across some of the country's harshest land. Unfortunately, one of the men who works on the fence is not available to interview, so I'll have to return to catch up with him another day.

From Tibooburra it is 335 kilometres south to Broken Hill, our next major destination, where I'll interview a number of people. So what is between here and The Hill? Well, I had a whole heap written, but then decided that you need to find out your own way in your own time. So I deleted it.

'Road-kill?' – the road south to Broken Hill.

Now, you really wouldn't want me to spoil all the fun for you, would you? You need to investigate, to explore and to get a sense of the outback your own way. Either go out there and find out for yourself, or read up about it, in travel books or on the internet.

But let me give you just a brief glimpse.

Anything you want to know about explorer Charles Sturt, you'll find out here. This is his country – this is where he roamed and left his mark. There are many stories about him, and about goldfields and settlers, and all sorts of yarns of big sheep stations and more. A great place to see and start you own discovery is at Milparinka, population of just six, located 39 kilometres south of Tibooburra but 1456 kilometres northwest of Sydney. From Milparinka, it is a straight run south to places like Packsaddle Roadhouse and Slate Mines, and just 112 kilometres north of Broken Hill is Fowlers Gap Arid Zone Research Station. Part of the University of New South Wales, this working station draws students from around the world to study a variety of topics, including eco-tourism and, would you believe, road-kill. Yep, dead animals on the roadside.

Instead of driving straight through to Broken Hill, I camp on the side of the road, but hidden from it by a small hill and low bush, south of Packsaddle and north of Paringa. There are interesting country hills on the west and dry flatlands to the east. I watch the sun go down having a cuppa from my favourite tin mug, alone with the dark coming. Soon, only stars light the sky, and later, a sweeping spotlight far away to the south. Probably roo shooters. At last it's time for me to roll into bed.

'The Flying Doctor artist' –
Howard Steer.

BROKEN HILL

HOWARD WILLIAM STEER, ARTBACK ARTIST

'What makes a successful artist? Poverty, I guess. I've been there and I don't want to go back there.'

Broken Hill is a place that I spend a lot of time in and love. It has many faces. Built on mining and with a long history – it's the birthplace of BHP – it is also internationally known as an arts town. No one is more responsible for that than Pro Hart. Some of my time spent with Pro was written up in my last book, *The Bushies*. I lost my old mate and I still miss him greatly. He would be the first to acknowledge the other great characters of The Hill. I also wrote of Joe Daley in the last book. Sadly, Joe died just before Pro. I lost two old bush mates within a few months. Joe gave me a Talc Alf sculpture (more about Talc Alf later).

As tempting as it might be to devote a whole book to the people of Broken Hill, for now we'll look at the lives of just a few. This is real Australian outback country. They call Broken Hill 'the gateway to the accessible outback'.

There is greatness in The Hill. Many take it for granted and some in the arts field have now moved on. Not the man who is probably going to be recognised as taking over from Pro. He has always painted in the shadow of Pro Hart. They got on well – they were mates. They never boasted of their work, but both knew they have given the world something to enjoy. Pro has now gone to the eternal campfire, painting still. Near him, I imagine, is Chips Rafferty, another Broken Hill born-and-bred man, reciting a scene from a film; Henry Lawson and Banjo Paterson are writing; Slim Dusty is serenading them all; and more and more will join them. Great Australians.

Who is the man that has stepped up to the mark to keep Pro's town alive? Howard William Steer.

A number of words come instantly to mind when talking of Howard and his work – words like whimsical, irreverent, historical, larrikin, bloody funny, and, sometimes, a touch controversial.

Howard William Steer is a born-and-bred outbacker from Broken Hill. His father was a powder-monkey in a quarry; his great-grandfather a miner and mayor of Broken Hill; and 100 years later his brother, Ray was deputy mayor.

Howard is one of those people you occasionally meet who has a weird sense of humour. He has taken that inbuilt humour, added it to his talent as an artist, and become very successful.

'Don't just be another pigeon on the roof,' he stresses, 'create an identity. Create *your* identity. Nolan did it with his Ned Kelly paintings, Drysdale did it with his outback pubs and the battler images.'

Howard has done it with his famous Flying Doctor – the caricature man dressed in black with a hat, carrying his doctor's bag and flying with white wings – which is included in most of his paintings. He is known as 'the Flying Doctor artist'. He has also raised over $212,000 for the Royal Flying Doctor Service over the years.

A self-taught artist, Howard was surrounded by art as part of his job. But let's go back into his history first.

'Born-and-bred Broken Hill-ian. My maternal grandfather was Irishman William Driscoll, who was a miner at Rockhampton, then Cobar and finally Broken Hill. He was mayor here between 1912 and 1916.

'My father, Lance Oakland Howard Steer, was a powder-monkey at the Australian Blue Metal Quarry in Broken Hill. Mother was Myra. Both of our parents are buried in town. The children include my sister Brenda (born 1943), then me (1947) and younger brother Ray (1950).'

Howard went to St Peter's and St Paul's Primary School and then Marist Brothers College in Broken Hill before leaving at fifteen to work in a wood yard cutting wood – 'bloody hard work'. Then for nearly three years he worked in a dry-cleaning factory, as he couldn't pass the medical examination for mining due to his poor eyesight. In 1964 he got a job working as a 'pen pusher' for four years with the SA Brewing Company, doing stock control, warehousing, counting kegs and being an 'all-rounder'.

'The new Entertainment Centre was built in 1970 and so with sixty-four other applicants I applied for a job and got it, as an all-rounder I guess, caretaking, doing all the locking up, etc. In 1971 our son Andy Robert was born. He's a chef, married with a son, Bayley. They live in Adelaide. And then in 1974 our son Jay Travis was born and now he's an artist living in Adelaide too, with wife Karen and kids Alicia, Kaila and Gage.

'My job at the Entertainment Centre developed into the manager's job as he was sacked. I looked after the bar and was the light and sound technician. The main conference centre had a 1000-seat auditorium and included the Regional Art Gallery, so I was also hanging art, packing and unpacking art, and setting up exhibitions. You don't realise what you learn at the time, but I did learn a lot seeing all the different varieties of art.

'I learnt that you didn't have to be a professional, but just have a go. I thought, What a great hobby. I was a non-drinker, non-smoker, and just decided to have a go at art as a good hobby. I don't know how I became an artist – I just dabbled, had a go. I looked at the different styles. I started giving away paintings to family and friends. I did a lot sitting in an old tin shed. I'd give one to anyone who called in, but they'd leave it behind when they left, so that may say something of the early ones!

'I had over 600 paintings – did them on masonite, packing cases, anything that was flat. I even would paint on something to add to a leaking wall or whatever. Then I finally sold a painting through Joyce Condon's shop in town. She was a local artist and seller. Her shop has always been a gallery. My brother Ray now owns the shop and runs his own gallery, Art on Argent.

'That first painting was called *Hot Air Balloons Tangled in My Mind*. Most of my paintings have had a story. In fact I called myself a story artist. That first painting sold for $350 and was sold to a pub somewhere in New South Wales. Joyce gave me the first opportunity to hang work commercially. She went on to sell about four a week for me in that shop.

Howard's work and reputation as an artist grew, and he successfully combined painting with his job at the Entertainment Centre. However, tragedy struck him down one night, changing his life forever.

'I had the accident in 1992. During a performance on stage a curtain weight 58 feet overhead fell and hit me. It took two of my fingers off and badly damaged a third one on my left hand. Somehow I managed to get two towels from the kitchen and bandaged it and made it to the back ramp, where caterer Ken Holden noticed me and raced me to the local hospital. It was locked and he was banging on the door. I was in a lot of pain. Finally, they got me inside and put needles in my arm, but realised it was too bad, so Flying Doctors, at 2 am, flew me to Royal Adelaide Hospital, but they couldn't stitch the two fingers back on. I was in hospital about a week, and again later when they did grafting and fixed a cut in my arm. Finally I went back to work – they kept me on for four months but then made my job redundant. That was in 1993. Six months later they were advertising for my position, but with the qualifications they included I wasn't qualified to do my own job.'

At forty-five years of age Howard had a lot of living left to do. He'd never been on the dole, and never intended to be, so it would be a case of living off his savings, but luckily he owned everything – no debts. And that was the start of a new direction in life.

'I still remember the look on my wife's face when I told her I'd been made redundant. She just said, "Let's sit down and have a cuppa tea." Now, looking back, it was a bit of a godsend really; she'd been through the trauma of the accident and all that. We decided to write to all art galleries in Australia and see who liked

'Art as a good hobby' – Howard and Lyn Steer in their gallery.

'A lot of sitting in an old tin shed' – the artist's domain.

my work and who didn't. I'd already won major art prizes and had sellout exhibitions in Sydney and Melbourne, but it was always hard trying to work and do my art. Anyway, we decided we'd give it a go.

'We worked out we'd need a typewriter, photostat machine, guillotine, a ute. All up $42,000 was spent in setting up. I did a course on matte cutting, taught myself frame making and then we started producing art for Australia-wide. Within twelve months we started to see some results. We had put a lot of thought into how we were going to do it all.

'It was three years before we won the court case for the accident that cost me my fingers.

'After the court case, by 1996, I was doing four or five exhibitions a year in Sydney, Melbourne, Brisbane, Adelaide and Perth. Then I got involved in combined exhibitions in London, Paris and in regional areas all over Australia. I painted up to about thirty or forty paintings for each. I also became heavily involved with raising money for the Royal Flying Doctor Service.

'I started to do a range of cards, and that made people more aware of the Flying Doctors. I'm now up to card forty-three, and when we reach number fifty I will change direction with them a bit. The Captain Sturt card, for instance, is now into its third printing – 10,000 each print run. I originally couldn't even find a publisher who was interested, but finally Peter Nicholson of Watermark Publishing took it on. We've been printing for seven years now, distributing all over Australia.'

In 1996 a bunch of Broken Hill painters became the next generation to follow the *Brushmen of the Bush*, that famous art group consisting of Pro Hart, John Pickup, Eric Minchin, Hugh Schulz and Jack Absalom.

'The Arid Zone Artists' included Howard William Steer, Shane Gehlert, Kym Hart and Geoff Demain. They, too, would achieve widespread recognition in the Australian art world, not only as a group but as individuals.

'Then in 2001 I was approached by artist Paul Blahuta about doing something for the Year of the Outback, 2002. He wanted to do a series of outback-oriented works, so we did something a bit different. We agreed we'd both paint on the same artwork together. He'd do the background colours in Sydney – fifty paintings – and then we'd meet in Broken Hill and work together, painting on the same painting. The galleries didn't like the idea much and when they asked who painted what, I'd say I did the upstrokes and he did the downstrokes … they really didn't get the idea.

'Actually, he'd do the outline of something and I'd finish it, then I might do some trees and he'd do the buildings or whatever. We just kept swapping over. I might be using a hairdryer on one painting while he was painting on another, and then we'd swap. It was the first time galleries had something like it and they were not impressed and couldn't see how they'd sell them.

'It was in 2002 that we formed Blood Brothers [the name used for all Steer–Blahuta collaborations]. Anyway, we showed the works in Collins Street Gallery in Melbourne with a series called *The Return of Burke and Wills*. We dressed up as Burke and Wills and left the explorers' statue and walked with three camels through the city to the gallery. It cost us $650 to "park" the camels at a carpark for two hours. We had 300 people turn up at the gallery and we sold $100,000 worth of paintings before the show finished. Of the fifty paintings, we sold more than half. So much for the lot of negativity of other galleries.'

As well as doing solo and Blood Brothers exhibitions, Howard continued to exhibit as a member of Arid Zone Artists. Also in 2002, Blood Brothers did a Ned Kelly series they christened *Paying the Kelly Brothers a Visit*.

'In 2003 we had a series called *First Australians* in Adelaide, and also one called *BHP Mining*, shown at the Stock Exchange in Perth.'

In 2004 Howard did a solo show for the Flying Doctors in Perth. As half of the Blood Brothers, he also worked on the *Celebrate Australia* series, which was shown in Singapore and sponsored by the Australian Government, and another called *Captain Cook*, which was shown in Sydney.

'After having painted 250 paintings together, we have never had as much as one cross word. We send drawings to each other initially and discuss back and forth our ideas as "templates" on a series – we know exactly what we are going to paint even before we start. We do a lot of research about the subject, find out the facts that may not be generally known, and try and put that into paintings. When Paul comes here we work sixteen to eighteen hours a day for about six weeks. Sometimes I go to Sydney but most times he comes here.

'One series we are working on is *The Law Courts*, all about being innocent before being found guilty. We like to do something historical, to pass on history to the next generation. We usually work on about four paintings at the same time. Nolan did seven paintings on Burke and Wills; we did fifty. Next will be a series called *The Cricketeers*.'

Howard is represented in many art galleries around Australia: at Waltzing Matilda Centre in Winton, which has the painting *The Drover's Wife*; at regional art galleries like Swan Hill, Dubbo, Broken Hill and Lake Macquarie; and even at the Stockman's Hall of Fame in Longreach, Queensland. His *Bush Olympics* painting was featured on Channel 9's *Sale of the Century*. He was also invited to add to the famous Arthur Boyd murals on the bar walls of the Tibooburra Hotel, so he did two promoting the Royal Flying Doctor Service.

His work has been featured in magazines and books like *Dog's Life*, *Kendall Country Connections*, *Expressions*, *Land Rover Experience*, *State of the Art*, *Contemporary Artists of Australia* and *Australian Art Collector*.

Many well-known people have Howard's art in their private collections. People like US bestselling author Jackie Collins (who bought sixteen works), former South Australian premier John Bannon, former deputy prime minister Tim Fischer, former governor-general Bill Hayden, former South Australian arts minister Ann Levy, former politician Clyde Holding, trucking magnate Lindsay Fox, country singer John Williamson, artist Ken Done, musician Don Burrows, as well as Coca-Cola and the Southern Imperial Corporation in Chicago, USA. One of his works also hangs in the boardroom of the Royal Flying Doctors Service (RFDS), Sydney. He has done many works for RFDS, in Toowoomba, Adelaide and Broken Hill. Over the years he's donated to charity a number of painted items, such as miners' hats, bins lamps, even a poker machine. He's painted about three-dozen miners' hats – one raised $13,000 for the Queensland Variety Bash.

The list of his achievements goes on and on. He has been extremely generous in his charity work. A pity then that someone within RFDS decided to send a letter demanding he stop using the Flying Doctors logo, stating that they owned the rights to it. He received an apology, only to be once again approached by them about trademark infringement. Negotiations continued and finally they realised he was doing them a big favour. Perhaps they needed to look at how much this man has raised for them and how dedicated he's been to their cause for many years. Having donated $55,000 to RFDS from a project I instigated with Pro Hart and not even received a letter of acknowledgement, I too question their response to the generosity of Australians who work to assist their cause.

Finally, after thirty-five years as a painter, how does he see his work now?

'I've taken an image and taken it to the next level to be recognised in the arts field. I guess for me it is the umbilical cord to the outback. I termed the phrase that I'm an "art-back artist". If you've got a dream to paint your dream. Take it to the full extent you possibly can.'

THE BROKEN HILL RABBIT TRAPPERS' UTE

In 2006 I put forward an idea to the head of tourism at Broken Hill City Council, Fiona Ellis. She and the council agreed and I commenced work with Howard Steer to create the Broken Hill ute, as a follow-up to the one I had done with Pro Hart. This one would be different, though. Howard would paint scenes all over a 1970 HT Holden – an old bush ute that seemed appropriate for The Hill. I would take it to many parts of Australia to help promote the 'accessible outback'. In 2006 I was an ambassador for Year of the Outback, and was driving the country in an F250, specially designed and sponsored for me by Hema Maps, and towing an outback caravan. Both the ute and the van were highly decorated, the ute with outback scenes, the van with a huge portrait of Chambers Pillar, a spectacular feature about 100 kilometres up a dusty track south of Alice Springs that many tourists never get to see. They became the most photographed ute

'Shaded by an umbrella' – Howard in 42°C heat, working on the 1970 HT.

and van in Australia. The themed caravan idea has now been copied by at least two other companies that I know of.

It wasn't until February 2007 that Howard and I started work painting the HT. In 42°C heat, we set ourselves up outside his garage on the footpath shaded by an umbrella, and for the next week we would paint the ute. I hasten to add I was only Howard's apprentice, painting the bits I could, and leaving the real artistic work to him. It was good to have a series of daily lessons with a great artist. Watching Howard Steer – magic artist – at work was a joy. Soon it was all done and into Silver City Crash Repairs, where Lindsay and Pat Wilkins finished it off with a clear coat and heat-bake treatment and did a final clean-up. Straight away it made the front page of the newspapers and appeared on television. The ute was quickly booked to appear at many events, the first at Broken Hill St Pat's Races and then out of town at places like Bendigo, Ballarat, Canberra, Deniliquin and many more. It really is a great addition to my ute collection and a tribute to artist Howard and the City of Broken Hill.

How do I decide which subjects to interview or write about from a town that has had so many interesting characters over the years? I could choose any number of people; many of the ones who are now dead had a great story, but there are also some people who are very much alive that few know about. Another artist in town deserves a mention. He's almost the opposite of Howard Steer, who paints non-stop and I reckon is looking for a way to do it in his sleep as well.

'The most photographed ute in Australia' – a tribute to Howard and The Hill.

'So many interesting characters' – Broken Hill's never been short of them!

'Painting is his life' – Colin Warren.

STILL IN BROKEN HILL

COLIN WARREN, RABBIT SHOOTER AND ARTIST

'I always felt like the king of the world out in the bush, even during 52° heat, sandflies, swollen rivers, but also in the good times – the light, the whole deal.'

In contrast to Howard Steer, Colin Warren is an artist who is not well known. In fact, I can claim some credit in getting his work into a local art gallery. He was happy just to sell his limited-edition prints wherever and whenever he could. When I showed a number of people a print of his that I had bought, some even doubted he was from Broken Hill, as although they'd lived there all their lives they'd never heard of him. Colin won't sell his original paintings, but he's happy to share copies.

I knock on his door on the road heading south from the centre of town. He lives in a neat and tidy world, unusual for a man on his own. This is the story of someone who made a living out in the bush, long before he took up painting. Now painting is his life.

Colin Warren is an outbacker who has seen a lot of bush over the years. He grew up on a soldier settlement fruit block at Winkie, between Barmera and Berri in South Australia, near the Murray River. When his parents retired to Berri in 1960, Colin started work as an apprentice panel-beater at age sixteen, but it didn't work out. The wanderlust took a hold and he headed off to Queensland for eighteen months, just 'bumming around' as he puts it. He ended up in Rockhampton, but then decided it was time to return home to Berri.

He started work at Glossop for Grant Engineering, where he learnt to weld. Over a twelve-month period he was involved in heavy construction – shed framing and the like. He then really started to get the wanderlust again. His ability to weld got him a job in Adelaide and he bought a motorbike to help in his plans for travel. The job in Adelaide was at a steel pressings place, the first in South Australia to use MIG welders, making cross-members for Valiant cars.

'In 1964 I met a young lady called Noeleen at a motorbike race. I bought a new bike and joined the Phoenix Club and was racing motorbikes. I met her there – she loved bikes. She was sixteen, I was twenty. It was the days of rock 'n roll, jive dancing, and she loved to dance. I had a duck-tail hairdo, stove-pipe pants and all that. I was into Buddy Holly music. I was bat shit over his music, it was the most magic thing. I also like the Big O, Roy

Orbison, and country music as well. Not so much into Elvis then, but Noeleen was.'

The happy couple were married two years later. Colin swapped jobs as it suited him – it was easy to do so in those days when jobs were easy to find. He worked for various councils, driving road rollers, doing bitumen work. Noeleen first worked in a clothes factory, then a chocolate factory, and later as a waitress. 'She was always a good worker and never had a problem getting work.

'A mate enticed me to go on a trip to Melbourne in his truck, and that was the start of my love affair with trucks. Even though I was always a small bloke, I was determined I could do what I wanted and I finally became an interstate truck driver for two years. I was always driving from Adelaide to Melbourne and back. I loved it; but it stuffed me, wore me out and nearly buggered my marriage – that was the catalyst to go bush.

'My wife said, "Try the railways", so I got a job as a packer (or fettler) on South Australian state railways from 1970 to 1976, doing track maintenance out of Coomandook, where I also started to shoot rabbits part-time. It was a good sideline and ended up earning me more money than my railways job. I finally moved to Adelaide Railway Yards for a while.

'I had bought a 6 x 4 foot trailer and had a fridge on it. I would sell the rabbits into the pub bars around Adelaide. In one to one-and-a-half hours I'd sell between 200 and 300 pairs of rabbits at $2 a pair. When I first started work on railways at Coomandook I was earning $30 a fortnight and paying $5 a fortnight to rent the railway house. Needless to say, rabbit shooting became an attractive alternative.

'With the rabbit shooting as a sideline we could live like kings. With a bit of ingenuity and a bit of a get up and go I could see I

Still in Broken Hill

could change my life. I was a lackey, working for the man. I wanted more – to have a go, chase money. I had the ability, but I always got sick of working at the job. I was always looking, looking for what I wanted to do. I was jack-of-all-trades but master of none. With the rabbits I could see I could change my life.

'I moved to Peterborough with the railways as a trainee Class 2 engineer. I wanted to get closer to Broken Hill so I could go rabbit shooting up north. I'd been up the Dog Fence, and I had a view to get closer to the rabbits. I had a dream, but most people put me down and said, "You just can't do it, you won't make a job as a rabbit shooter." Finally, in 1977, I said "Stuff this" and I gave the railways away. We moved to Terowie and bought a house. I had a bit of station work, mainly with sheep. I loved station life. I did whatever I was asked – truck driving grain to Port Pirie, dipping sheep, loading hay, cementing tanks, fencing. I learnt a lot from the owner of the station, Hans Schultz.'

Colin worked on and off at the sheep station from 1977 until 1980. Between jobs he trained his own sheep dogs and for a few months a year would follow the sheep shearers, eventually getting onto a shearing team picking up and pressing wool. He loved the bush life.

'Noeleen was alone a lot of the time. Even though I loved station work, the money wasn't good and so finally we decided to make the break. I went to see Ted Cronin, a rabbit buyer in Broken Hill, about full-time shooting. I had stars in my eyes, and he said I could earn $300 a night – which of course wasn't exactly true. He got me onto Omocron Station, near Moomba. I was to work over the border in southwest Queensland, near Cameron Corner.'

So with stars in his eyes, and an old Land Rover and a tent, Colin again left his wife to go off and try to make their fortune.

'What a shock. I arrived on Omocron Station – it was a 52° summer day. It just felt like normal to sit in the chiller all day with the rabbits and drink water for hours. Late afternoon you'd open the chiller door to go and a sensation of the blast of heat would hit you. It was like opening a door to hell.

'Then we'd get ready to go shooting all night. Even now, all these years later, I still remember it. It was like the John Denver song which says "coming home to a place I've never been before". Another of his songs is "Sunshine" – all most relevant to our life. Since I lost my wife, all that is too confronting now. Many places I see between here and Adelaide particularly remind me of her, and I still find it hard.

'Anyway, after a while I really got into it and got up to 120 pair a night. The best I ever shot was 233 pair a night. We'd be paid $1.20 a pair back then. But it was always dependent on drought, rains and such. Sometimes you'd only get thirty pair a night. I

'Coming home to a place I've never been before' – loaded and ready to go.

remember one buyer sorting through the rabbits and picking out the best and we had to throw away as many scrawny ones as they bought good ones. That's the rabbit game in a nutshell: you need rain and good feed. When I left the railways I was on $500 a week. Then I was earning $1000 a week shooting rabbits. By 1991–92 I was shooting up to 200 pair a night on average at $1.60 a pair.

'We used to shoot the moon and then come home for a while – in the black – by that I mean the best time to shoot was three to four nights leading up to the full moon, when the rabbits were quieter, then a night or two after the full moon. Always the best time: you travelled less, the rabbits were quieter, you could see more and get in closer, and you used less bullets. I used a 55-watt yellow fog light then and could get about 30 yards from the rabbits. Later you'd get head shots from 60 yards out but with a 100-watt spotlight, which I used when I first started, but when a

'It was just magic' – another night's work on the rabbit shoot.

pro it was the yellow fog light. I rarely used a spotlight under a full moon, but always a really good telescope on the rifle. I started with a Model 2 Brno bolt-action rifle with a four-power Kales scope. Then I also got a Remington 17 centre-fire with eight-power Leopold scope, for foxes and feral cats for the skin trade. My last rifle was an Anschültz with a six-power Bushnell scope. A beautiful light little rifle. Over the years I had many guns. I reckon I've had about forty to fifty guns.

'As a professional shooter you go through a barrel every four to six months. In the sandy country the dust is a real killer. I'd bury the barrels or use them as a car jack. I would sometimes put 500 shots through the barrel a day, so the barrel and trigger action would suffer. Often you'd get new barrels and trigger mechanisms and just re-bed the old wood stock to suit and use the old firing bolts. For a professional rabbit shooter I reckon the Model 2 Brno and the Anschültz are the Rolls-Royce of cheap rifles. Serviceable professional guns. Anschültz was dearer but good.

'I found the sandhill country always good for rabbits – less miles to drive. I'd shoot for half an hour, then spend ten minutes gutting the rabbits and then start to re-shoot. In winter I'd shoot for an hour then start to gut. I'd always keep an eye on the time, always a set routine to shoot and gut. I was shooting six to seven months a year and then I'd do casual work for the rest of the year. The best year I had was when I earned $30,000 for a shooting season. For that sort of lifestyle it was just magic. I couldn't believe I was living that sort of great life. The last gutting was in early morning light, and I'd be listening to Roy Orbison on the wireless. It was just magic.

'Often Noeleen went with me, and we had the kids on correspondence school for a while. But then it was only during school holidays. I was mainly shooting the South Australian sandhill country. To get to the camp we'd follow the Dog Fence. I did all my own cooking. You'd take a big drum of water, a drum of fuel, a case of bullets – 5000, which in 1994 cost $120 a case.

'Finally, I gave it away at Christmas in 1994. I was at Billacalina Station, near Roxby Downs, and we heard about the calicivirus that accidentally escaped. "Accident" be buggered. Within days it was in Queensland and we knew our industry was buggered.

'Myxomatosis is an airborne disease spread by mosquitoes, but calicivirus isn't and will wipe out an area (but not all). I don't know if any shooters are still out there now. I know when I first started shooting there were eight chillers and twenty-five shooters just on one station in three to four camps, depending on the size of the chillers. I haven't shot professional since 1994 and I don't know if any of the shooters are now. It's all too restricted now too. You just can't have a gun and go like we did back then. That idiot in Tasmania who shot people and the new gun laws stuffed it for us in the bush. It didn't affect the criminals; they still get guns.

'Out there in those days I felt like the king of the world out in the bush. I loved the light. Sunrise and sunset were magic. Even the bad times – the heat, swimming swollen rivers – the whole package. I didn't like the heat or the flies, especially the sand-flies after rain; the little pricks – they humbled me, they were so relentless they drove you mad. But still I loved the whole deal. In the bush I was king.

'After the years of rabbit shooting I worked for Outback Tours, driving as a tour guide to places like Mungo, Mootwingee, Mildura, Pooncarie, Menindee Lakes. I'd do my *Crocodile Dundee* bit to make it interesting – show them lizards, roos, emus and stuff. What I didn't know I made up. I did that in 1993 and then went to casual driving jobs for the RTA – driving water tankers, anything

'King of the world out in the bush' – another bush camp.

at all that was going on work-wise. I was starting to bugger up – riddled with arthritis, particularly hands and back, and that's what you get for being a smart arse knocking a small-framed body around all those years doing what I did. I'd also been out in the bush too long. I did a bit more truck driving, as being on the dole for me just wasn't on. Now, though, I'm on a pension, the arthritis has me. I don't know how much longer I'll even be able to paint.

'At the time when it really started to knock me around, Noeleen wanted to do foster care. She just loved kids, and all our three had grown up. It gave her a reason to feel good and it was like a new lease of life. We decided to give the poor little buggers a go, a start in life and some stability. Geoffrey, he was here at the age of twelve, he had a real tough life. His parents were drug addicts. We gave him as much as we could, but when he left here and went to Adelaide he was stabbed at only sixteen and died. We had a lovely little baby at another time. We had about nine kids here all about, over a period of time.

'Noeleen got sick in June 2001, and the following month, in July, she died of leukaemia. She had a blood clot develop from the chemotherapy and had an aneurysm.'

The loss of Noeleen affected Colin greatly, and he says he hasn't got over it. Everywhere he goes reminds him of her, and he misses everything about her. He was depressed and it was art that helped him a lot.

'I first went to Robinson College to do a beginner's course in art in 1993 for six weeks. I only went because a friend was doing it and asked me to come. I enjoyed it, but then I went back bush and to the rabbits. However, later the same year I joined Willyama Art Society, just for something to do. My stuff was crap, but I had a go. I started to put my art into Willyama exhibitions. People liked them and they started to sell, but just at amateur prices. Everything I've ever done I've sold [save for the originals, of course] – that's over 300 sold. Prior to my wife dying, they were selling OK and getting to a stage where I could sell at higher prices.

'When I lost Noeleen, I threw myself into art. Everything from then on in art, it became totally different. Art gave me a reason to keep going when I'd lost what meant so much to me, losing Noeleen was just so bad. Art has given me a dream; it's so important to have a reason to get out of bed each day. I don't want to change the subject matter of what I do in art, but I want to do different aspects. I want to expand my art with special effects like shadowing and moonlight work. I just want to expand my horizons, not just do commercial stuff for money.

'I want to explore – do something different.'

'Art has given me a dream' – Colin with two of his artworks.

I have to start up the ute and head west to yarn with another character of the bush. It's only a half-hour drive, so don't worry, you'll have plenty of time to take photographs and wander around this historic town and see where Australian and overseas film and television companies love to come. I've been there many times and after a few beers and a toasted sandwich at the pub we'll meet our next creative outbacker. This bloke is a character with a bush sense of humour and an unusual talent.

We will return to Broken Hill, as I want to introduce you to more Hill-ites, just to show you that in one town in the bush you can really spend a lot of time with great people. Broken Hill is one such town; throughout its history, it has always had interesting people. Take the time to dig deep in any Australian town and you will find wonderful history. But first we go half an hour west of The Hill to Silverton.

'I can make $150 from a penny' – Andy Jenkins.

SILVERTON

ANDY JENKINS, COIN CUTTER

'The fun part is I can do it – no one else can do it legally.'

Travel west of Broken Hill for 23 kilometres on a tar road that has more ups and downs than the big dipper at Luna Park, and you'll find the historic town of Silverton (1881). You know you are there when you pass the camels on your right, go through a final dip (which is the Black Hill Creek) and then see old peppercorn trees on both sides of the road.

In the early days, Silverton was a busy little place. It created an Australian first on 12 January 1888, when the Silverton Tramway opened for operation – the first privately owned rail company in Australia, linking the South Australian line with Broken Hill via Silverton. But by 1899 the Municipal Council ceased operation, leaving the town in the control of the New South Wales government. The village is now managed by the Silverton Village Committee, which is made up of the local population and two government departments.

Immediately you are struck by the fact that way out here are some pretty well-built and restored brick and stone buildings. They add strength to what may at first look like a near-deserted town. Keep on past the old gaol on the left (built in 1891), which now serves as an excellent museum, where you'll find out that this was once a more substantial town. The museum is a credit to the local historical society and well worth a visit.

An interesting aspect of Silverton is that no one pays rates on their properties and there are no services like rubbish bin collection. It is a town no one wants to be responsible for. Land that was once leased but not owned by people is gradually becoming available to purchase outright.

Finally, on the left you will see the Silverton Hotel, famous around the world as a set for countless movies and television commercials. Turn left up the dusty track past the pub – but don't forget to make time to call in for a drink, some tucker, a yarn and a gander at the photos of movie life on the walls (ask if you can take 'the Test').

Just to prove how much film companies love to come here, the following list shows some of the many movies and TV commercials that have been shot in Silverton. Films include *A Town Like Alice*, *Mad Max 3*, *Razorback*, *Outback Bound*, *Dirty Deeds*, *Fiddler's Green*, *The Craic*, *The Golden Soak*, *Ring of Scorpio* and *Blue Lightning*; and TV commercials have been made here for local and international companies like Eveready Batteries, Carling Beer, XXXX Beer, Coffee Mate, Icegold Beer, British Lions and others.

'Home away from home' – Andy's Coin Carvery, Silverton.

The Silverton Hotel has appeared on screen under many names. Here are some of them: the Nullagine, Hotel Australia, Gamulla, Mulga Mulga, McInally's Ridge, Digger's Rest, Chuck's Diner, Martinvale, Juanita's Diner, Starbreak Station, Federal, the Mundi Mundi Hotel (three times), and even once as Wally's Tea Rooms.

Righto, that's it. Time is running out and the sun is high and hot.

On the left, a few hundred metres away, is a less than impressive building. Not your elegant brick and bush stone, but made from another great material nonetheless: corrugated iron. The tin shed has a large sign that simply says 'The Coin Carvery'. This is the home-away-from-home of Andy Jenkins, who has created a name for himself as a coin cutter or carver. It's grown from a home hobby to a full-time and well-known business. He has about 30,000 visitors through his studio each year and sells his unusual coins all over Australia.

Andy was born in Broken Hill in 1949. His father was also local born and his mother came from Adelaide. His father was a sheet-metal worker in the mines, and his grandfather was a miner, as were all his uncles. Andy left school at fifteen in 1964 and first worked at the John Windham Bicycle Shop in town, mending bicycles, washing machines, televisions and such. He earned £5 a week.

'The lure of big money a few years later led me to the mines,' he tells me, 'and by the age of about nineteen to twenty I went onto shift work at the treatment plant for three years, and then with electricians underground. When I was still under twenty-one I was finally accepted onto the staff of the mining company and stayed on until 1982. I worked in the geology department as a prospector and underground sampler, and later above ground as a drill-core sampler for North Broken Hill. I was retrenched in 1982 and then offered another position with the company, which I stayed in for eight years, as caretaker of Queen Elizabeth Park. It was in the City of Broken Hill but sponsored by North Broken Hill Mines, and I was there until 1990. I also had a tip truck contract as well. It took me until 1990 to work out what I wanted to do. By then there were fifteen work trucks of ex-miners around town and I could see I could make more money another way.

'It happened this way. You see, in 1976 I went to America and at the Los Angeles County Fair I bought an Aussie penny cut up by a Mexican. I thought, I can do that. So when I got home I practised over and over and eventually it became a very successful hobby for me. I had given away a lot to my family and friends and then people started saying, "If I give you a penny, can you cut it up for me? How much would it cost?" It went from there, and from 1990 I've been doing it full-time – I work seven days a week to keep up with orders. Tourists don't have days off.'

Initially, Andy had a spot at a local Silverton gallery and set up shop there in 1990, but in 1992 he finally asked an old man if he could discuss buying the tin shed. 'It had a sign on it for $10,000. I told the old man I could not afford to pay $10,000 for it. He said, "What do you mean? It's $2000!" Seems the old man had told his son over the phone to put up a for-sale sign on it. The son had mis-heard the price and so the shed had sat there from 1983 to 1992 attracting no buyers, until Andy came along. They agreed on the sale, so next day Andy broke the lock with a screwdriver and moved in. Then he settled in and has been there ever since.

'It was built in 1983 as a shed for the Back to Silverton [barbeque] and never used after. It was made from old scrap stuff they found around the place. I raised the roof by 3 feet to get the cooler in. Putting in a heater and town water cost $3300 and power cost me $5000. We don't pay any rates.

'Silverton is un-incorporated. No council, no mayor. Not worth it; there's only about fifty people left. We have town water from the local reservoir and power is supplied from Broken Hill.

'It was finally the Lands Department that came in and reclaimed a lot of the land. There's no land available to buy, and my place is on lease but perpetual, and I've applied, and should get full title next year. Then I can build on it if I want – but I won't. I will probably just add a bit more security around. In winter it's cold and in summer it's hot. We've had tornadoes go through, but I reckon the wind just blows through my place here, whereas airtight places just explode. I have a wood heater with a manifold on it that pipes hot air onto my feet to keep warm when I'm working. The cooler works good too.'

Only half of the shed has a raised roof to 10 feet 6 inches and the long cooler pipes flow nice cool air around, but walk under where the roof is only 7 feet 6 inches and, boy, don't you feel the heat! Luckily, we did the interview sitting below the cooler. It was 43°C!

'It's not an excellent business, because I'm here seven days a week. Five days would be good. But I'm not on the dole and I pay all my bills.

'A blacksmith could move in and it'd already be dusty for him. In fact I had one who wanted to buy the place.' Andy has a dry sense of humour that creeps up on you unexpectedly.

Like a whacker, when I first met him I said what thousands have said to him before when they see all his pennies around the place. 'Haven't got a 1930 penny, have you?' (They are very rare and worth many thousands of dollars – the prize of prizes.) What a stupid thing to say to a man who has thousands of pennies ... If he did, do you think he'd tell us or sell it on the spot to a tourist?

Sometimes, no matter how hard we try not to, we become a stupid tourist. I reckon the brain knows when you're on holidays and it goes into dumb mode. I always try hard not to go into dumb mode as I'm on the road a lot, but I fail sometimes.

A bit later during our interview I mention to him how dealing with tourists must require great patience. He has a trick for the person who asks that question about the 1930 penny, and here more of his sly humour comes to the fore. 'When someone asks me if I have a 1930 penny – and they do – I just say, "Yes, I do. It's over in that glass case over there." They're really surprised and go off to find it among the hundreds of coins. I altered one to read 1930! It shuts them up pretty quickly.'

I thought this was a good way to react to that question he's always asked. I tell him I have the halfpenny in my collection that's worth the most, but no 1930 penny, sadly.

Andy's dry humour also comes into operation whenever some (mainly old) women look at earrings but procrastinate over buying them. 'They get out of it by saying, "Oh, I'd like to buy them but I don't have pierced ears." So I reply, "That's OK, ear piercing is free", and point to the big paper punch on the wall. I even offer to do nose piercing for free too,' he laughs. 'You got to have a bit of fun.

'I don't need patience to do the job but I do need perseverance. I can put it down any time and walk away, but you have to persevere, as you have to catch up on back orders all the time and have stock on hand. It takes half a day to cut out one penny, or three-and-a-half to four hours.

'I tell the dumb blondes I can do it quicker in winter,' he says

'You've got to have a bit of fun' – ears pierced for free!

with a smile. 'They ask why and I tell them the days in winter are shorter!'

What Andy does with his pennies is this: he painstakingly cuts out the blank bits, leaving only the main design of the kangaroo, the year minted, and the words 'Australia' and 'Penny'. He does something similar with dollar coins.

'There's silica bronze in a penny which goes through the blades, so to cut out one penny uses up about ten blades in the handsaw. Then I get them gold plated in 24 carat in Adelaide. I cut out only the kangaroo pennies that run from 1938 to 1964. I take anyone's birth-date year and will supply them if I don't have it in stock, but they have to wait. I post out free anywhere in Australia. A one penny done this way costs $150. So you see, I can make $150 from a penny,' he grins cheekily. But, of course, once you take out his time, the cost of gold plating and getting the pennies to and from Adelaide, and supplying the customer, his

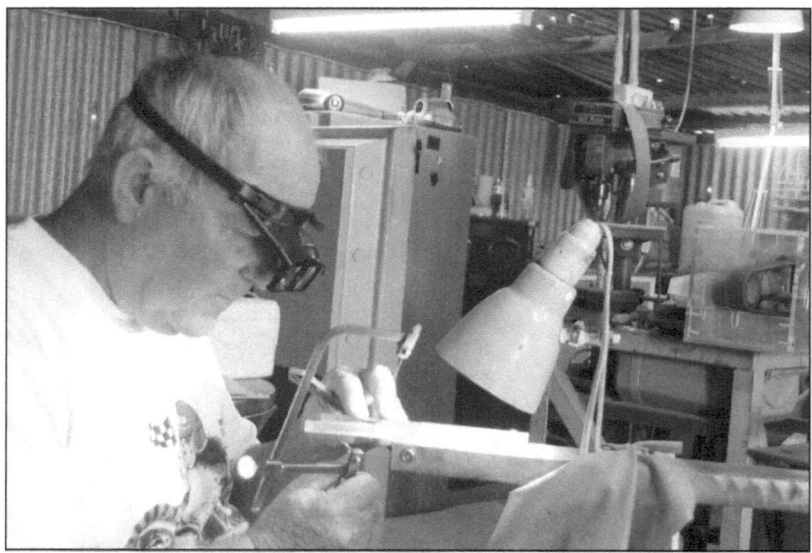

'No one else can do it legally' – hard at work.

profit is reduced. He can make a good living by not selling wholesale.

'I sell predominantly to Aussie tourists in busloads and individual cars. Very few Asians come out here. Word of mouth seems to be the best. I often get someone buy here, and then I get faxes or phone calls from their friends to post stuff. I'm a member of a wholesale group, Australian Gift Homewares, and once a year I have a site at the trade fair at Homebush in Sydney. It gives me exposure. Soon I'll have a place on the sea where we have a holiday home – then I will spend winters here and summers there.

'The $1 coins are by far the most popular selling,' says Andy. (Even though I will leave later with a little bag of coins, I forget to buy the $1 one, so I'll have to get one next time.) I notice at his feet are large plastic folders containing pennies. 'One family sold me 6000 pennies in one go,' he explains. 'Basically new 1938 to 1964 kangaroo pennies. They wanted 25 cents each for them, but in the end I got them a lot cheaper than that.'

Andy also has other coins he's created. He has both sevenpence and threepence halfpenny. Post-decimal kids are going to get lost here, but you oldies who know the old currency will follow where we are going. Still, I have to explain that the sevenpence is made up from a penny with the centre punched out and a sixpence inserted in the middle using a one-ton press. The threepence halfpenny is made up of a halfpenny with the centre punched out and the hole filled with a threepence. They are then polished, ready for sale.

Now, don't get ahead of me, folks. I know what you're thinking: what does he do with all those punched-out centres from the penny and halfpenny coins? Naturally, Andy thought of that long ago, and for $12 you can buy copper buttons with two holes in them made from the punched-out centre of pennies. They even read 'one penny' on them. Sixpences, threepences and pennies and halfpennies may no longer be accepted currency, but they are still in circulation thanks to Andy's efforts.

'People who buy the penny buttons use them for all sorts of craft and artwork. They get a card of them with six buttons for $12. One bloke from Melbourne was using them as decoration for shoes, another on clothing. They're good to do your trousers up with, a fashion statement – and they never wear out.'

Any leftovers from the fine works all get packed up and sold. The fine scrap dust that comes off when sanding the coins clean contains a lot of silver and is gathered and sold as scrap. You see, Andy is also proud of the fact that much of the silver in them was originally mined at Broken Hill. So he likes to think that not only is he creating great Aussie art pieces out of the silver and bronze coins, but he's also selling Broken Hill silver.

Andy can have copies done of any coins that are not available, and these sell either in silver plated or gold plated. They range from $35 to $50.

The work is very detailed. 'Every time I put a penny in, the challenge is to finish it. About six a year I stuff up and about fifty to sixty a year fail – they delaminate and fall apart. Concentration is the key. You can't let your mind wander or go on holidays while you cut. The biggest frustration is keeping up with orders in winter. Tourist time is basically Easter time to November.

'I also have permission to cut out coins from France, Greece, United States, Singapore and Ireland. They also come in sterling silver or gold plated. I cut out an original and then cast them from a mould of the original. The silver for them comes from the same refinery that uses Broken Hill silver. They sell for $30 to $50.'

It is this 'permission' that I'm particularly interested in. I want to know how he got permission – was it very hard? The sly smile on his face tells me I'm in for a story here.

'From when I started it was two-and-a-half years to finally get permission from the Treasurer. First, I wrote a letter to the Mint, and they didn't even bother to reply. So I assumed they had accepted it.'

As you would. I'm a great believer in assuming you have permission until someone tells you different. Usually then it just stirs up a hornets' nest of bureaucratic bullshit and red tape. Anyway, don't get me started on how this country has become swamped with a bunch of tossers in power wanting permits and payment for anything and everything and nothing. Back to Andy.

'Apparently they finally passed my letter on to the Department of Public Prosecutions, who wrote to tell me to "cease and desist" and even added a date by which I had to do it. So I got legal advice, but kept on doing it anyway. I think I was the first and they intended to make an example of me. They sent a bloke out from Sydney to Silverton from the Department of Public Prosecutions – and let's not put the full details in here of how I found out, but I believe he had a warrant in his pocket and came into the studio to catch me out "destroying government property". He never introduced himself as to who he was or what he wanted.

'I showed him a penny already cut and still attached to a saw as I usually do, and did my talk. He never actually caught me in the act of cutting and "destroying" a coin. He didn't say much and left. Anyway, let's just say I was then told who he was and what was happening, but no need to say how … He's still probably wondering how I found out, and he would be amazed. Let's put it this way: another bloke came into the studio after he left and we discussed it.

'With that, my lawyer wrote a letter which basically discussed entrapment and gave them two weeks before we'd proceed. We received permission for me to use the Government Copyright and to destroy government property exactly two weeks – and one day – later.

'I then asked for permission to use the design on the one-dollar coin. My lawyer thought I was pushing it a bit on that one, but I said, "What I have I got to lose?"

'Paul Keating even rang me, and basically he wanted to discuss royalty permission, but I said I was already paying 31 per cent wholesale tax. We discussed other stuff, and eventually he said a letter was in the mail. The permission was only for me to use; I couldn't train anyone else and I couldn't sell the business. Then the police Currency Crime Squad from Sydney got in touch with me and did an investigation and checked some stuff. Now, they are very good blokes and they always like to check re fakes, so they ask me. Every artist is identifiable.

'The fun part is, I can do it – no one else can do it legally. Yes, there are others around that do it, hobbyists who mostly go through markets and such. I know most of them and where they are and what they do.'

As an example of another cutter's work, Andy then shows me some coins that have coloured clear silica on them.

'He got permission because he proved that what he does doesn't "destroy government property". He can simply melt the silica off and it returns the coins back to original, whereas I actually cut the excess bits from the coin and just leave the

'I'm a paperboy every Sunday' – more sly humour at play.

artwork. The Federal Police have shut down people and taken them to court. One bloke keeps reappearing, though, and they get him.'

I ask Andy if there's anything else he wishes to add about his work. The reply comes with his usual wit.

'Yeah, my other job is that I'm a paperboy every Sunday – I'm on the end of the line of the world's longest paper run. The Sydney *Sun Herald* and *Sunday Telegraph* actually are allowed to come out on the one truck from Sydney. A tonne and a half arrive in the morning and I pick it up about 10 kilometres out and deliver them to five newsagents for them to deliver in their area. It's a *Herald*-owned run, and I was told by the *Herald* it's the world's longest newspaper run. Unique in that sense, and apparently it's the only one to carry the *Herald* papers and the *Telegraph* on the same truck all the way. I've been doing it for twenty years.'

Tourist customers have been coming and going as I interview Andy, and it is time I went too. After taking a number of photographs of Andy at work, I can see some more customers coming up the dusty track, so we agree to meet again soon. It's stinking hot outside his place as I take the final shots, after which we go inside and I pack my camera gear away and collected my stuff together. Andy and I shake hands as four people enter the tin shed.

As I depart and am a few feet from the door and again blasted by the sun, I overhear a loud old bloke say to Andy, 'Haven't got a 1930 penny, have you?'

I can't believe it. How many times has Andy heard that? I smile to myself, and even more so when I hear Andy reply, 'Yes, there's one over there in that cabinet …'

I couldn't have written the script better myself. I'm still smiling as I get into the ute. I just can't believe it.

Stupid bloody tourists!

Well, as the sun is getting low in the sky, we may as well stay on a bit longer. I want you to see a great sight – the sky. I see there's a heap of clouds, and that is great. That is the best sky to have when you view the sun setting over the Mundi Mundi Plains. Later, in darkness, we leave Silverton and, forty dips in the road later, we are back at Broken Hill.

'Pride and dedication' – Bobby Shamroze.

BROKEN HILL TO ARKAROOLA

BOBBY SHAMROZE, PROUD AFGHAN HERITAGE

'All I ever wanted was to achieve something for recognition of what my father, grandfather and other Afghans did in the outback during the pioneering days, to open up this great country.'

In a back street in Broken Hill one of the first mosques built in Australia remains as a place of worship for the descendants of the original Afghan camel drivers. The red corrugated-iron building has date palms around it and the interior now is restored. Zaedulla Fazulla, grandfather of Bobby Shamroze, was one of those camel drivers.

'Camel team business' – grandfather Zaedulla held numerous roles in the community.

Few people in Broken Hill would know that the name on Bobby Shamroze's birth certificate is Ammin Nullah. Most people just know him as Bobby. He also answers to the nickname of Bindi. His brother Ramah Tulla is known far and wide as Rocky.

Their father was Shamroze Khan (known as Bob Shamroze) and their maternal grandfather was Zaedulla Fazulla. Their maternal grandmother went by the name of Crasha Maude Nohab. Needless to say, the Shamroze family tree is an interesting one, with a variety of names.

Grandfather Zaedulla came to Australia in the late 1880s from Attock (then in British India, now in Pakistan) when he was just seventeen. Known by many as Abdul, Zaedulla had fourteen children. For a number of years he ran his own camel team business in the west Darling – from Broken Hill to Wilcannia in the east, up to Tibooburra in the north and White Cliffs and Wanaaring in the northeast, down to Wentworth in the south, and to many other places. He carted gear from the mines, and would backload wool to the railhead. It was a general carrying business. When times were tough Zaedulla would load camels with merchandise and hawk his wares around the back-country stations, where he was most welcome. As he grew older he became sick with asthma. Finally, he gave it away in August 1925 and ran a small shop until about 1937, when he became too ill. Son Abdul took over the business in the 1960s and used trucks. His first truck was a 1960 Commer. Lance 'Bull' Steer (artist Howard's father) worked with Zaedulla for a while also.

As well as being one of the last practising cameleers, Zaedulla became one of the community's religious leaders.

'Grandfather Zaedulla was also the butcher for all the Moslems,' Bobby tells me now. The cattle had their own special brands and the meat was always kept separate. He would cut it up according to strict Moslem tradition. I helped bury him in 1960.

'Highly respected' – Zaedulla's son-in-law was the great Bejah Dervish (third from right).

I had to wash his body. He was the last Indian mullah – priest – of the Mohammedans [later they became known as Moslems]. He was ninety when he died. Grandmother had died in 1949.'

Zaedulla had become a successful businessman, and the Fazullas were highly respected in Broken Hill. (One of their daughters married the son of Bejah Dervish, famed member of an exploration party in Western Australia in the 1890s.)

'My father was Shamroze Khan and my mother was Miriam Bigum Fazulla. They were married in 1932. He had arrived from the hills of Pakistan in 1894 when just seventeen, like my grandfather Zaedulla. My father first worked in the smelting

'Religious leader' – an Afghan desert burial.

'I cannot eat jam at all now' – Bobby as a boy (right).

works at Port Pirie until he saved some money and then went to Melbourne, where he started and built up a hawking business. He bought drapery and other goods and then hawked it all around Victoria.' He was also a camel driver in the early years.

In about 1928 Shamroze Khan arrived in Broken Hill with a sizeable bankroll and continued to trade as a hawker. He and Miriam were married four years later and soon people knew him as Bob Shamroze. He wanted to be recognised as an Australian and, similarly, his children became known as Bobby, Rocky and Rose.

Bob Shamroze became a very successful businessman and owned many residences in Broken Hill, which he rented out. Some years before his death he lost a considerable fortune due to the malpractice of a businessman he had trusted. He became a gambler, attending the races (he and his wife often won the best-dressed couple prize at race meetings). In about 1935 Bob Shamroze took a job aged fifty-seven as a surface labourer at the Central Mine. His last job was shovelling coal for the Silverton Tramway Company, which he did until the day before he died of a stroke on 8 June 1952. A beautifully made and embossed coat, well over 100 years old and worn by him as part of religious ceremonies, has now been restored in consultation with the Sydney Powerhouse Museum, and thanks to the Shamroze family is on display at the Migration Heritage Museum in Broken Hill.

Miriam had left Bob, a much older man, when Bobby was just four years old. Bobby was born in 1940 and remembers life being very tough growing up.

'After she left, we lived in a corrugated tin shed – just one room with dirt floor, a double bed with two blankets and old army coats to keep warm. Just two bricks on the floor was where the cooking was done. I had one set of clothes. All we ate was hot curries and bread and jam. I cannot eat jam at all now. I remember someone gave me a pair of pyjamas. I ran around outside in them as my clothes. Even though we owned houses all around town, we lived in a tin shed. I lived like that between the ages of four and eleven.'

Other people have good memories of the Shamroze family. Artist Howard Steer, who grew up near them, says they were a good family. 'Bobby's father was too generous and trusted everyone. He was very well liked in Broken Hill. The kids did it tough.'

'I just refused to go to school in Broken Hill and always wagged it,' Bobby continues. 'At the age of twelve. I had got into a bit of trouble in Adelaide and I was put into a boys' home from twelve to fourteen-and-a-half. Then the principal said, "You can go now." I was then sent to Straun Farm School from fourteen to fifteen-and-a half. All I had was a Grade 4 education.

'Straun Farm School was at Naracoorte, an experimental farm. They treated me real good there. I learnt to shear there. There were nineteen boys and we all had a different job. We were taught skills, and we would be sent to work on other farms as well. I learnt to milk cows. Finally my grandfather and uncle came and got me out of there and brought me home to Broken Hill.

'In 1956, aged sixteen, I went to work in my first shearing shed as a rouseabout on Kinchega Station. From there on I worked in sheds like Glen Lyon, Grassmere, Rednan, Mount Lyndhurst, Mount Poole, Mount Browne, Mount Wood, Olive Downs, Pinkellie and Waterbag. I didn't do much shearing, but some. I was mainly on the wool press. I became a gun presser, could do forty bales a day.

'In 1960 I married Janet, who I had met at Naracoorte.'

Janet tells her story at this point. 'I had to run away from home to be with Bobby. I was just seventeen and my family wouldn't have anything to do with "that black South African", as my father put it. Anyway, we took off and got to Adelaide. We had no money and had to borrow enough to get the bus to Broken Hill. My father never spoke to me for sixteen years. We arrived here with nothing and struggled but were able to get some help to get started.'

In 1964 Bobby gave the shearing away and started work in the mill of the South Mine for six months, then went underground as a trucker. In 1965 he moved to the Junction Mine, hand-trucking underground, and also doing scout mining, but the mine closed in 1972, so he went back bush.

'I went wool pressing for six months, then worked as a labourer at the hospital for three months, and finally got a job at the South Mine, working as a miner timber stoping between the 900-foot and 1400-foot levels underground until 1972.'

Bobby went back to Junction six months later and worked there as a miner until 1974. He then put his name down at the North Mine, but they said there were no jobs.

As he was leaving the office, he ran into the underground manager (who he knew), who told Bobby he could start work the following Monday. He again installed timber underground for six years and then, as he had his first-aid certificate, he ended up on staff as an ambulance rescue officer between 1980 and 1989, when he had to take a forced retirement package. He then worked for MSS Security for fourteen months before fully retiring. But fully retired doesn't mean much to Bobby – he still works.

'I go bush and help mates on their stations, with sheep and anything else they want. I also fiddle about doing up a house for a grandson. I mainly work on two stations, Yackawina and Munka, both just about 50 kilometres from home.'

Bobby bought the old corrugated-iron house next door to his own. They call them 'tinnies' in Broken Hill. He has two large sheds and garages and is a bit of a 'hoarder', as he puts it. He has numerous cars for restoration, and a 1958 Ford Mainline Star Model ute is the current project, and it's looking good. Everything around the Shamroze family home shows pride and dedication to their lifestyle. For a young bloke brought up in a rough old tin shed, Bobby admits he's come a long way. The home has many, many photographs of family, of many generations. It is an extremely neat and comfortable home, not just a house, and I sense the couple's real but quiet pride in their family.

'Sixteen years after I ran away from home with Bobby,' says Janet, 'my father wrote to me and said, "Bring yourselves and whatever children you have and come visit", which we did. Dad recognised he was wrong and we made up. He became extremely fond of Bobby, idolised him in fact, and knew we were good together. They spent a lot of time together and we looked after them in their old age until they died. Bobby has always been good to me and he's the best thing ever in my life.'

The Shamrozes are now grandparents. Of their three children, Debbie has twins, Julienne has three children and son Randall has two daughters.

'We've been very lucky – all our kids still live in town and they and the grandchildren are great.

'Life has been pretty good since I met Janet,' says Bobby. 'I used to drink a bit when a shearer (most do). I never smoked and haven't had a drink now for twenty-five years.'

Bobby is good with his hands. He has done most of the building around the place, and he's also built a holiday 'shack' on the water at Copi Hollow. The kids have a place there as well – built by you-know-who.

Now sixty-eight, Bobby still waterskies and owns his own boat and caravans. His grandchildren also have him on rollerskates. Something tells me his days as a busy man are well planned ahead. I can't see him sitting down for too long, although I think he enjoys just doing what he want when he wants.

I've enjoyed my yarn with Bobby and Janet. Interesting history, and when Bobby and I wander around his two blocks and share an interest in 'old stuff', I feel I get to know more of him and his life. He can be proud of where he's comes from and where he is now. Tough young lives sometimes can go one of two ways – he chose the right path.

It is time to leave Broken Hill again. I reckon I have approached or left the town by every dirt or bitumen road at some stage or another. I never tire of spending time here. Today it's up bright and early and I'm heading west, the day much cooler than recent ones, although it could be hot by lunchtime in The Hill.

(As a postscript to this story on Bobby Shamroze, in June 2007 the Islamic Council of New South Wales presented him with three specially inscribed plaques dedicated to his grandfather, his father and himself 'in appreciation of pioneering work in the service of Islam and Muslim communities of New South Wales'. They were also installed on the honour board in Sydney.)

YUNTA: THE BACK ROAD TO FLINDERS AND BEYOND

I fill up with fuel at the service station at Yunta, about 200 kilometres west of Broken Hill. There, I run into the Yunta postie, who has a great ute, but won't sell. His wife reckons he'll sell her before his ute. His daughter agrees.

I have a cuppa and a sandwich and hit the road again, but not to the west; this time it is back onto dirt and to the north for a long way – all the way to the Strzelecki Track. This is the back road to the Flinders and Gammon ranges and other great spots, a road not normally used by tourists. Be sure if you go this way that you have plenty of petrol and supplies, and don't come in wet weather or with a caravan. You're a long way from anywhere most of the time.

Before you get to Frome Downs, you can head west and end up at the Flinders Ranges, but it is advisable to check track conditions long before you do as there are some rough patches at times. Always check if rain has been anywhere in the area before leaving any bitumen. Yunta is always a good place. Local people know conditions, especially the mailman.

Along a dirt road, about 140 kilometres northeast of Yunta, near the southern edge of Lake Frome, is Frome Downs Station. This is where Australian actor Alec Wilson lives, but you don't just rock up to his doorstep and expect a welcoming smile. He is sick of tourists and four-wheel drivers who cross his land and drive along the Dog Fence, using it as a short cut to the border. You can't blame him, it must drive landowners crazy worrying about what damage they'll find next on their properties. Some tourists leave rubbish, campfires burning, gates open, and camp beside the only stock watering place around for miles, and then they wonder why landowners get mad.

People soon find out trespassing isn't the done thing on Frome Downs. Wilson is well known in the district. You may remember him in *The Anzacs*, *Cool Change* and the *Crocodile Dundee* movies. He looks the part when he plays the baddie.

'We won't be visiting him today' – Alec Wilson's place, Frome Downs.

The sign near his place says it all. I haven't made an appointment, so we won't be visiting him today. I'll ring well ahead next time.

Not far past Frome Downs Station you skirt the edges of Lake Frome. At one point, you will see and cross a straight road, which has signs on it at various locations saying not to use it. This is the gas pipeline road, which runs all the way north to the Moomba oil and gas fields and south nearly to the Barrier Highway, not far from Peterborough. Let me point out one thing. This is a long, straight road used by people in a hurry to get somewhere either north or south. But if you decide you are going to use it, be warned that trucks go to and from Moomba on this road – they won't slow down if they see you, and you'll soon find out what they think of you being on 'their' road. Many people have found out the hard way. Broken windscreens and coughing dust for mile after mile isn't nice. It can be a dangerous option to go on this

'Coughing dust for mile after mile' – heading northwest to the Gammon Ranges.

road, especially if you tow a caravan. I would only use it in an emergency, although I know some people ignore that advice and run the risk anyway.

I'm now at the back of the Flinders and heading northwest to the Gammon Ranges. I've had a slow and lazy day today. I decide I will camp out tonight, and tomorrow night stay at a room at Arkaroola.

THE BUSH SINGS

I awake to the sound of a nice bird call. I can't see the bird, but it's in a nearby eucalypt and its melodic call rouses me. The sun is just about to poke its head above the horizon. I am a bit stiff from sleeping in the swag because there's a thin layer of white frost on the entire length of it. I didn't feel cold during the night, which says a lot for the quality of the old swag. It's canvas, and long ago I coated it with waterproof spray. I love my old swag, which I bought in the late '70s or early '80s. Sure, she's a bit dirty, but she is still a great bed and I always throw her in the ute; she goes wherever I go. People don't realise that while it can be hot in the outback during the day, at night it can be very cold. I am in a rocky gully, large eucalypts abound. I am alone, well off the beaten track, a small sandy creek nearby – I'm enjoying the morning.

I light a fire. Soon the smell of smoke hits my nostrils as I throw on some dead eucy leaves gathered from the base of a tree. They are slightly damp from the frosty night, so I've pulled a small piece of bark from a tree also. You don't need much, it is always dry underneath, and a little bit will soon have a fire crackling. But never strip a whole heap off a tree, because (a) you don't need it, and (b) if you do, you may be destroying the retreat for spiders or other tree dwellers. Look before you strip, and take only a small piece just to get the fire going.

Tiny twigs soon catch alight once the bark has some flame to get the damp leaves going. Damp leaves will burn fine, but expect a bit of blue-grey smoke. That's OK – that first hit of bush smoke is just one of the experiences in the bush. Make sure you learn not to have a continually smoky fire, though, as it will drive you nuts, especially when cooking. Me, I've been doing it for years and I always love to create a fire without smoke, even if it's raining. Some people build humongous fires for no reason other than they think they have to.

A small fire causes no dramas and will warm you on a chilly morning; the coals make a great spot to put the billy or frypan. Man, I love early mornings in the outback – it comes alive and soon more birds welcome the day, as the sun creeps high and makes a splash on the ground through the trees.

'Enjoy the experience' – good to see the gate's shut.

This is a great time: warm hands by the fire, the bubbling of a billy or the sizzling of whatever takes your fancy for brekkie. I love bacon and eggs with cold tomato and, of course, tomato sauce. The bush – what a wonderful experience it is, I never tire of its charms. The feeling of being with nature. Hot tea in an enamel mug tops off a great start to the day. Lungs fill with cool, crisp air and the growing warmth of the sun invigorates you. What simple pleasures it brings; it's something you can never get sick of. It makes you feel alive.

On really cold nights and if you are sleeping on the ground, two small fires can make it seem much warmer. Just like toasting on both sides at once. At the end of the day, before dark, collect a heap of dry wood and some small twigs to rekindle the morning fire. Sleeping between two fires not only keeps you warm on both sides as you roll over, but if you are with a group of people often you'll need two fires anyway to allow for a lot of cooking. But if you do sleep between fires, make sure they are well apart and that nothing is within reach of them, especially your swag, bed clothing or whatever else is flammable.

Enjoy the experience. Don't expect or want total comfort like at home, with the ducted heating and percolating coffee machine doing the work for you. Seems some people can't live without their home enjoyments. The day I see someone making coffee from a machine on a sand dune in the Simpson Desert is the day I leave the outback.

Enjoy a bit of roughing it, learn to take in the sounds, smells and sights that a new morning brings. My lungs always feel better out in the bush than in a home. The more you try to enjoy, the more great sensations will arise. Listen like you've never listened before; close your eyes and you will be amazed at just how many sounds you can hear, close by or in the far-off distance.

'A joy to watch' – as long as the snakes keep their distance ...

The bush sings.

Well, to those who listen, anyway.

Tiny lizards are a joy to watch. I've often sat having a hot cuppa or breakfast in the early morning in the outback, just sitting cross-legged on the ground. Let your eyes focus on nothing in particular, but just take it all in. Sooner or later, out of the corner of your eye, you can often pick up the movement of a tiny gecko darting between the ground litter, leaves, stones and such. I've sat and watched their antics many times, these inoffensive, tiny, but important members of the bush. When you sit and look at a full-sized sand goanna or perentie lizard some few feet long, then it is even more amazing. They are just the most incredible and graceful animals. I love them. Snakes and me, on the other hand, are like non-speaking neighbours; we avoid each other as much as possible. Snakes too have their place in the bush, so long as it is not near me. I had too many close encounters as a kid that

'*A slow and lazy day*' – all's quiet around the windmills.

coloured my feelings and I've never changed. Lizards, goannas, geckos and more, however, can come into my camp any time.

Just remember one thing: goannas can become very tame and will eat from camp sites. Many drovers and bushmen years ago had goannas they could hand-feed. If a goanna becomes alarmed, however, the first thing it will do is to achieve height, by climbing the nearest tree, and they might not see the difference between your trouser legs and a eucalypt. They are extremely fast movers when they want to be – don't be fooled by that slow casual walk they usually have. Their claws are extremely sharp. Don't get too cocky with what looks like a tame goanna. Their bite could also have you reaching for a brandy to calm the jitters, not to mention the first-aid kit. But they are absolutely brilliant to watch at close quarters.

ARKAROOLA: OVERNIGHT STOP

I stop overnight at Arkaroola resort, 600 kilometres north of Adelaide. With its amazing rock formations and crystal-clear night skies, Arkaroola is a place where geology and astronomy go hand in hand. Study the ancient rock formations by day and look at the stars by night. Many professional and amateur rockhounds and stargazers come here to do just that.

But it's not just for experts – tourists come to explore these ancient wonderlands, and there are bushwalks too. It is a remote area (mobile phones may or may not work) and much of it is traversed in four-wheel drives. However, you can certainly wander here in a normal two-wheel-drive vehicle, or simply pay to join one of the many back-country tours. Be warned, though: tours aren't cheap, especially if you have a tribe of

'Where geology and astronomy go hand in hand' – Arkaroola resort.

ankle-biters with you. The resort isn't cheap either, but the pub serves great meals.

I could write a great deal about this place, but we are just here overnight and there's no time to go exploring too far. Again, I shall return one of these days.

A warm day lies ahead. It's onwards for me. Up through the ranges, down through dry, rock-strewn creek beds, beauty surrounds me ... this country gives me a deep sense of satisfaction. Through station gates, over stony tracks, red dust and changing flatland. I wander from the ute every now and then and go exploring along creek beds, photographing all sorts of stuff. I am taking it slow and looking at many things – one track led me miles off into unknown lands – but I always find my way back to the track I'm supposed to be on. My advice is always carry good maps, be very sure of where you are going, and leave signs.

'Ancient wonderlands' – a wall map at Arkaroola.

Soon I am back on the track, heading northwards to my destination. I have directions to where I need to be, I just have to find the people I'm after. They gave me bush directions: 'Look to the left of the track before you reach the Strzelecki Track around the Mt Hopeless area …'

It is late afternoon and I spot a camel, then another; and soon I see, off in the distance, a large wagon, a Land Cruiser – and people. We've met before and it will be great to see them again and their amazing collection. Here on a plain with areas of red stone. This will be my home for the next few days.

'Work, patience and total commitment' – Gill Wheadon and Kye Crow (and friend).

MT HOPELESS

KYE CROW AND GILL WHEADON, CAMELEERS

'Live the life you love.'

Up until the middle of last year, my previous experience with camels was that they were usually on the other side of the fence, frothing at the mouth, bawling mournfully and looking like they wanted to rip your arms off. So being snuggled, smooched and generally loved mercilessly by nineteen camels all trying to meet me at the same time was an experience I will always remember. One of those unique memories of my time in the Australian outback.

To say that those camels I first met in 2006 on Calcutta, an outstation of Mt Lyndhurst Station in South Australia, were different, is an understatement. These were all once abused and badly mistreated animals until rescued; and what gentle loving creatures they became due to the work, patience and total commitment of their new owners, animal lovers Kye Crow and Gill Wheadon. At that time in mid 2006, the camels were resting for a few months on the station after a long, arduous journey, and would soon be on the move again, heading towards the Darling River in New South Wales and up into Queensland.

Kye and Gill are an amazing couple with total dedication to animal welfare. When I met them at Mt Lyndhurst, they had just walked from Alice Springs with nineteen camels, six dogs, eight chooks, one rooster, two corellas, one sulphur-crested cockatoo, two pigeons and a donkey – as part of their own sort of vision quest to find a home where they could live in harmony with their animals and do their life's work.

Imagine doing what they did. After twelve months' planning, you sell your home and give up a 'normal' life in a town with friends. You sell all your belongings at five or six garage sales, build a wagon from scraps you found around the town tip and backyards – a wagon that looks like Noah's ark on huge wheels – turn your back on society and walk into the desert with animals that have been badly treated by humans. On top of all that, you don't know where you're going to go, except south somewhere … Well, that's exactly what Kye and Gill did.

Now, in 2007 many months after that first meeting, I'm at Mt Hopeless to see them again. In the meantime, they've conquered the desert and walked down the old Ghan railway line, down the Oodnadatta Track to Marree and onto the Strzelecki Track – some of the toughest country you can find anywhere.

Very few people in society step outside their comfort zones, security of employment, home and family. Generally speaking, society now finds excitement on the television watching others rather than participating. But there is much more satisfaction in participating at any cost than leading a life of quiet desperation.

Kye was born in Bromley, England, in 1959. She came from a very English middle-class background.

'Mum was the twin-set-and-pearls type. We had the biggest house in the street. My adopted father spent weekends at the yacht club or on holidays by himself on his yacht in the Greek Islands.

'My mum, Brenda, has always been an animal lover and rescuer. I remember once she bought an abused animal off a man, then cancelled the cheque to teach him a lesson. He took her to court, but she won. Mum said she was going to make him pay — so then she'd sneak onto his property and steal hay from his shed to feed the animal he'd abused. We helped her drag bales of feed across the paddocks in the dark. So even as a kid I was taught by my mother to rescue abused animals,' says Kye with a laugh. 'Mother gave me the love for animals, I remember sneaking into the cupboard with her to feed a little squirrel. We grew up with horses and dogs. I don't remember ever not doing it, I've been doing it all my life.

'My ancestry background is Irish, African, Jewish. My birth father I met when I was thirty-three; I grew up with Mum and my adopted father. I found out I was related to the Fanti tribe in Ghana, West Africa. I went to school at Tunbridge Wells, near Bromley, and later left school to work as a nursing assistant for the mentally and physically handicapped. Over the years I worked as a postwoman, a cycle hire attendant, a waitress, but I always felt I was never treated very well.

'One day I heard on the radio you could get £500 to start up your own business. Before I knew it, I was being interviewed on

'Doing it all my life' – Kye began saving abused animals as a child.

the BBC and in newspapers about my business – I was restoring cane and rush seating in antique chairs. I taught myself out of a book. I ran it for a year, but fell in love with an Aussie and ended up coming to Australia a year before the America's Cup.

'I lived in Fremantle and worked in restaurants. My boyfriend's mother was awful and we ended the relationship after six months, so I went around Australia on my own. In Brisbane I lived with lots of people I'd met. Finally, after returning home for a year, I came back and applied for permanent residency. I went to Cairns and stayed for seven years. I started to make clothes and sell them at the markets, I also did waitressing jobs, but I decided I wanted to create my own income. I got some white clothes and hand-painted them and they all sold. I wanted to sew my own clothes, so I bought a sewing machine and off I went. I met Gill in Cairns. Eventually we moved in together and were living on a beautiful peninsula, but six weeks later the house burnt down and we were standing naked in the street. We lost everything. When Gill arrived to move in he had a little green bag; by the time we left, all we had were two little green bags. We lived on communities and all sorts of other places. We've been together thirteen years later this year.'

In 1993 they lived down south for a while, then back to FNQ, and a scungy place in Townsville. 'Let's go to Broome,' suggested Gill, and five days later they were in Western Australia, where they stayed for five years, doing markets down as far as Albany, selling their hand-dyed garments. They spent a season in the Darwin markets. They had a truck loaded with their wares, and employed a lady to sew for them for about four years. Wunjo Crow Clothing was a good business. They travelled to Melbourne selling, and then back to Cairns. Business was good wherever they went.

'We did well from the clothing business, but it was time for a change, and now instead of wholesaling, we just sell direct on eBay. One lady alone has bought over fifty dresses and tops from us. I love to sew, I'll always make clothes. Gill is good at dyeing too. When we are travelling, we don't put anything on eBay, but if you just search "Kye Crow", you will find us when we're selling.'

Back in Cairns, though, they'd got sick of living out of the truck while looking for a new house, so Gill said, 'Let's go to Alice Springs.' So they did.

'We've always lived a different lifestyle to most,' notes Kye.

'I was born in the '60s in the western suburbs of Sydney,' says Gill. 'Mum [Helen] and Dad [Chris], four sisters and me. Dad was a boilermaker by trade, but he got fed up with it, so went back to school – and became a librarian. Dad died when I was sixteen, Mum is remarried and living in Bowral. I went to Ryde Christian Brothers and after finishing school I worked in timber yards as a yard-hand and then as a sawyer. I later worked on building sites. In 1986, when I was eighteen, I was sick of Sydney and so packed my bags and left. I worked on trawlers and reef boats out of Bowen, Queensland, then worked on cattle stations as a stockman at Croydon up the Gulf, worked in kitchens, picked tomatoes, was a dairy-hand on the Atherton Tablelands … I sold coconuts, de-nuted coconut trees in Cairns, did wood-carvings and sold them, and I picked bananas – one of the hardest, dirtiest jobs. Very hard on the back.

'Then when I met Kye we did all sorts of things, as you know, and thirteen years later we're still doing it.'

Gill is pretty handy. He taught himself to weld and the wagon they travel in is his own creation. And I gather it was Gill who came up with the plan for their big adventure out of Alice, but Kye was right behind it all, even though she was scared.

'I was, particularly when we sold our house on 5 acres, just outside Alice Springs. We'd settled and been there six years, but the cost of feeding all of our animals each week was larger than our mortgage. We really had to do something. I had the cheque for the sale in my hand. Looking at it, it was really scary to think we were going to use some of the money to go bush. I was really frightened but very excited at the same time. We were on a treadmill at the time and both so unhappy. Gill wanted to travel – I just wanted a home. We were working so hard, we were like a factory knocking out clothes. We spent New Year's Eve discussing everything and knew we wanted a change.'

'We'd had no experience with camels,' Gill admits. 'We just bought two and walked them 90 kilometres back to Alice one day. A friend of mine, Rick Hall, had camels, and did wagon work; he took me out bush once. You don't "get" camels – they get you.

'I bought a book on how to work them. Rick Hall inspired me with the wagon. He is a most notorious cameleer. He once was charged for being drunk and disorderly whilst in charge of a camel wagon. It was thrown out of court, though, as his defence was: he wasn't in control, a fourteen-year-old girl tourist passenger was.

'For Christmas 2001 we went to buy the two camels – and the man who we bought them off was being dragged around the yard like a rag doll by one. He kept saying, "He's a good camel, just needs a bit of work." The two young camels scared the hell out of us. On Christmas Day we were walking them towards Alice and there in front of us a corkwood tree had been decorated as a Christmas tree.' They both laugh now at the memory.

'A magnificent bunch' – hitting the road; destination Queensland.

'I had a vision ... no plans' – Gill eyes the horizon.

'At the end of the first day of travel the male camel, Neville, just collapsed, so we said, "OK, so we'll camp here then." Neville and Caroline are both still with us.'

Gill then began to outline his plan for the new (mobile) home they were soon to need.

'I had a vision of what I wanted to build, but no *plans*. I just built it – mainly from scrap, from wrecks I found in the bush, stuff from the tip, all over the place. I taught myself to weld; I wanted the wagon to be warm and dry to go through the bush, so I built a potbelly stove from junk. I wanted bigger tyres, to make it easier for the camels to pull over rough terrain. Basically, it was to be a big bedroom on wheels. I also wanted to add water storage tanks underneath (700 litres capacity), a cupboard under the bed, a small fridge and a pantry. It had to be able to carry six months' supply of food.

Of course, large solar panels were added to the back of the wagon on the roof.'

As he says, Gill knew what he wanted, and over many months it began to take shape. 'It took twelve months to build. I did the body, sides and roof, but then decided it was too big; then I thought, No it's OK, but then again no ... I knew it was too big. I was worried it wouldn't even fit through gates. I had so many things to think of. Finally, I chopped it down in size, took 2 to 3 feet off the height, and shortened it by about 4 to 5 feet in length. And it's skinnier now by 2 feet, so it fits through gates OK.'

Kye adds, 'You should see how he works. All this stuff lying around everywhere, and you wonder how he can do anything. But then he just gets into it and he creates. He's amazing.'

'I work on the chaos theory, and up comes an idea,' laughs Gill. He continues with the particulars: 'The floor pan I got off an old caravan – I modified it with an axe!

'Like Noah' – arrival at Marree was the highlight.

'The axle and Ellis wheel hubs set-up is off an old truck "spider" trailer. I had to modify it as well. The tyres I had trouble finding until I saw a Unimog four-wheel-drive tourist bus in the street one day. When I had a closer look I saw they were 20-inch, and so I found second-hand tyres off a Unimog with pretty good tread.'

Kye again adds her thoughts. 'Gill became totally obsessed in its creation. Quite crazy, in fact; he would sit there staring off into the distance. He was always thinking and planning what he was doing. I was quite terrified – how would we do it? I was very insecure about giving up our home. Gill was just totally excited.'

Gill again: 'I knew I needed to build it comfortable for her.'

Kye: 'We discussed it all the way, and talked about animals and what we'd be doing – and then I got really excited.'

'I felt like Noah. And when we got the white dove, it was all so very biblical.'

And finally they were ready. Or so they thought.

Saying goodbye to their friends, they left Alice Springs and headed down the old south road, towards Chambers Pillar. It was August 2004 and in the first month they only managed to travel 75 kilometres!

'We were having to learn as we went. We knew little about handling camels, how to even hitch them up properly. Only two or three camels would actually work for us at first. Plus, we had brake problems and we needed a new axle. We ended up getting to Deep Well Station and camped for six months until it got a bit cooler. Then on 23 March 2005 we took off again – following the Ghan rail line down as far as Finke, then to the Oodnadatta Track next to the railway line, and finally onto the Oodnadatta Track itself. It was then we started to meet all the tourists. Most were just lovely people.

'At Hamilton Station, Wayne and Janet were just amazing to us. At sunset we'd pull up and they'd turn up with a fully cooked meal. Spare parts they arranged to be flown in and delivered. They were marvellous. Then Vincent and Julie from Mt Sarah Station – they too were just great. All great people.

'One tough old station owner, though, was so emotional, he said, "I hope you guys get everything you wish for." He then turned away as he was all choked up. Amazing.

'Some people founded it too confronting – they just couldn't handle it when we'd say, "We don't know where we are going." They just couldn't believe it.

'We talked to lots of people who stopped. I didn't like talking to cameras that didn't talk back, though. Some people can be very rude. We had many cameras pointed in our faces before any response came from the owners. People just did their own thing. We'd always get asked the same things; we just wanted to get people thinking about camels.'

Some 1300 kilometres later, they were resting at Calcutta, which is where our paths crossed for the first time. I asked them what the highlight had been so far on their great odyssey. Kye and Gill agreed it was their arrival at Marree right in the middle of an Afghan Cameleers Reunion. They both gave excited responses at the same time, but basically the story goes like this:

'To see so many Afghan people with turbans on their head as we approached, with the camels and wagons and all the other animals … We were their vision coming out of the wilderness. There were TV people there filming, people were saying how we couldn't arrive at a better time. It blew them all away. For us to have that welcome was the big highlight. They surrounded us and presented boxes of fruit, meat and such. One lady was crying, saying how much we had impacted on so many people. Tourists just stood there you should have seen the stunned awe on people's faces.

'A wonderful end of the Oodnadatta Track for us.'

The sun was setting fast in the dusty west at Calcutta. As we spoke about that triumphant arrival at Marree, Gill noticed what was over at my ute. 'That's Blossom and his best mate Bella the donkey,' he said. Blossom had settled down next to my ute in the shade and the donkey was sniffing around also.

'Blossom was an orphan – we got her when she was a week old. She was dehydrated. She's hooked up and is best mates with Bella; they hated each other at first, but now they are inseperable. She doesn't go off with the other camels, she just remains near Bella all the time.'

A short while later, Gill noted that the camels had arrived out of the bush and were drinking down near the dry riverbed at a stock trough. 'Let's go and see them,' said Kye immediately. 'They haven't been around for a day or two.'

So we climbed into the four-wheel drive and headed down there. I was wondering how they would react. In the past my experiences with camels had been less than positive, remember. Little did I realise what a memorable meeting it would be. The camels came around as soon as they saw us pull up, and greeted Kye and Gill.

But then it was obvious they knew I was someone new, and they wanted to check me out. I was a bit apprehensive when they made a beeline towards me. Soon I was surrounded and being sniffed and snuggled by a few of the beasts – how friendly and

'A big bedroom on wheels' – the camel wagon that Gill built from scratch.

gentle they were.

'This is Alice,' Kye announced, beginning the introductions. 'She was born in the Todd River while her mother was giving camel rides; a tourist noticed something coming out. She was passed around to various people. Someone there owed us money, so we got her as payment of the debt.

'Mozee here came from the meat yard – he was too skeletal to kill for meat. He was the quietest animal I've ever met. He was a wild camel, but he just walked up and I led him home. He likes to sit and not move.'

Another camel stuck its face right up to mine and sniffed gently. Kye continued: 'That's Monkki. He was in the worst state when we got him – hairless, sores, mange, skinny – but he survived and now he is turning into a giant. He was an orphan and he's very quiet.

'You don't "get" camels – they get you' – Kye and Gill learnt as they went.

'Andaria came from Hemannsburg Aboriginal community, an orphan. She's very, very smart. She often takes over young camels and mothers them. She even stopped other young camels from chasing a car and led them back unassisted. She's amazing and one of the boss camels.

'Caroline – or Lady Caroline, as she's also known – is a bit aloof. She works well for Gill, but she looks at me and then him, almost saying, "Oh no, not the hired help again, Gill." She took four years just to acknowledge me. She's a great worker and a boss.' She did have that attitude about me: sniffed and, once satisfied, walked off.

'That one drinking is Kushy. She was an orphan we got from an Aboriginal community. A white camel that's gentle, slow and laidback. Not a good worker.

'Kunkaa – Aboriginal for crow. She's a young cow, unhandled, and fought us all the way. We smothered her with love to win her over. She's still a drama queen.

'Janti, she's a young cow, just six months old. Hadn't been handled, but after two weeks she decided we were OK.

'Oh, he's Rockhole, a Ross River bullock,' Kye said, pointing to Janki's neighbour. 'He's highly strung, a bit flighty and hard to handle.

'Zoo – a bull bought as a bullock. He was our first wild camel and a very big, tall camel. He was destined to go for meat, but we saved him.

'Lulu, there feeding, is a fiery little thing. Very woolly, she gave birth two months after arriving. We milked her to feed Windy, who has been the most challenging: a long, hard, dangerous road. She went into shock. Her eyes were open and breathing but not moving. She has settled down on the trip now.

'Jumuna, named after the river that goes past the Taj Mahal –'

'When camels were being loaded she wouldn't,' Gill cut in. 'She freaked out, put her head through the gate, lifted it off its hinges and took off. She was freaked out by the truck. She kicked me once. Not sure I wanted her, but Kye wanted her to be happy. She gave birth to Jali, a female cow now three years old, and Chocko, who's three months.'

At this point I spotted a big red camel, the biggest of them all, coming right for me.

'Here comes Abdul', Kye said calmly.

I was very much on guard. He was a huge red animal, a magnificent-looking beast, but I already knew his reputation and I was wary. Very wary.

'Snuggled, smooched and generally loved' – Gill with Lulu, at Calcutta OS.

Abdul pushed his way through the crowd and was soon towering over me.

Abdul is a legend. Even Kye said that when she first met him she thought, 'I'm not a camel person.' He was a very bad camel in his day. His mother had been shot, and the shooter noticed the stomach moved and cut Abdul out. A hard start to life, and Abdul grew up around the Oodnadatta Pub, terrorising anyone and everyone. Life as a pub curiosity meant he was often drunk, and knew aggression. He chased police around cars, chased kids and knew no rules. He would open the door of the kitchen and raid it of any food he could find. Abdul was a famous outback character. He terrorised tourists. Everyone was in total fear of him.

'He was finally taken to Alice Springs and we saw him in a paddock. He was going to be shot. We took him, and when people knew we had him they thought we were mad. They'd say,

"What are you doing with him? Are you are crazy?" But he is a legend and he's grown up and settled down. He's a boss.'

And here now was this huge, terrorising legend towering over me. He lowered his head and put his face right into mine and ... sniffed. So gently and quietly. I stroked his face and said hello. He was so gentle, curious and warm – a beautiful animal. He was interested and he knew his power. But he was so gentle.

I was being introduced to one and all, and now it was Gidgee who said hello. Kye continued the introductions.

'She is the daughter of Caroline, and Gidgee, too, gave birth while on the trip – to baby Posh, a cow who loves to travel. She's always the first one up each morning and first one in line.

'Adjani is an a Afghan name. She's a cow from Marree. She had been lent to someone and when she was returned she was very aggressive. When we heard of her, she was in a paddock, and she just walked up and I led her out. Now she's big, dominant, and doesn't take shit from anyone. Likes being boss. There's a pecking order in the herd and they've got to work it all out.

'The big thing anyone who has camels can't get over is that none of our camels have nose pegs and they're never led by the nose,' Kye adds. 'We just won them over with love.'

Finally, someone in the crowd decided it was time to leave, and when a boss camel leads, the rest follow. Soon a string of camels made their way across the landscape and back to the bush, where they were roaming and resting and 'having time to themselves', as Kye put it. The sun was gone as we stood in the darkening land and I was in absolute awe of the time we had shared. What a magnificent bunch of animals – all under the spell of these two devoted people.

Next morning I was up early and shared more time chatting with Kye and Gill until it was time to hit the road again. We promised to stay in touch, which is how we come to meet up on this later trip. I think I convinced them to travel the length of the Darling River up into Queensland, where they hope to eventually find a couple of thousands acres of land to buy and settle down with their 'family'.

Their long-term goals include saving abused animals. 'Animals are a big part of our lives,' Kye stressed during that first visit. 'They have so far saved about fifty animals in need. 'I suppose we are going to have to settle down for the sake of our animals. This trip is scary, sometimes real scary, but it's the most amazing experience of my life. I say to everyone, "Live the life you love."

There is no doubt that Kye and Gill have a huge commitment to their dreams, and I believe they will achieve what they want through their dedication and hard work. With Kye's love and passion and Gill's talent with camels and ability to have a go at anything, they make a great team.

'Our aim is to bring abused animals and street kids together to learn to love and trust again. And that will be a huge task, but one that we know will work.'

I stay for a few days with them near Mt Hopeless. A baby camel is born the night I arrive, and the next few days are interesting ones.

When it's time for me to go. I drive off into the morning sun, filled with admiration for these modern-day cameleers with their great animals of the Australian desert. They head off down the direction I'd just come. I make for where they'd come from – the Strzelecki Track.

I'm now a confirmed camel lover.

We met again months later about 100 kilometres from Broken Hill and spent a couple of days together. We also had lunch in

Broken Hill, and then they moved camp to Copi Hollow, near Menindee. At the time of writing, they are heading off up the Darling River. I've given them some road directions and hopefully they will get to share time with Warrego Woman (Andrea Rudd) at Fords Bridge. I'm sure the three of them have many yarns to share about their trips travelling with camels.

I've introduced Kye and Gill to my publishing agent, so perhaps one of these days their own book of life on the road will be published. In the meantime, have a look at their website: www.animalrescuecamelcaravan.com.

'Eccentric or just a free thinker?' – Talc Alf.

LYNDHURST TO SOMEWHERE UNDER THE SOUTHERN CROSS

TALC ALF, TALCUM CARVER

'I want to do something useful for Australia and pass on knowledge. It's to record the history – communication through the arts.'

A sandhill on the Town Common, Lyndhurst, South Australia. Population: 30 (most days).

I want you to meet the man who first introduced me to Kye and Gill, a man famous around Australia and overseas. He lives a couple of kilometres outside of Lyndhurst, at the start of the southern end of the Strzelecki Track. He was born Cornelis Alferink, but he is better known as Talc Alf.

'A camp off the beaten path' – the artist's home since 1974.

I'd heard much about him, seen him on television, and even had a sculpture of his in my collection. But I knew very little about him, and that annoyed me. Who was this man so well known for his sculptures and eccentric version of the alphabet? Was he really an eccentric or just a free thinker who rowed his boat his way? Well, I wanted to know more and was prepared to drive the best part a couple of thousand kilometres to find out. If he was eccentric, then all the better – great people to yak to, eccentrics. My wife says I am one.

Joe Daley, an old stockman from Broken Hill, gave me one of Talc Alf's stone creations some years before and I treasured it as a gift from a great old bushie. Sadly, my old mate died in late 2006. (His story is told in my book *The Bushies*.) Joe, a fan, like me, of Henry Lawson, also had a Lawson piece done by Talc Alf that I admired; I was determined that one day I would own one too. I fully intended to buy one from Alf before I left.

I pulled into Alf's yard on a sandhill a couple of kilometres out from Lyndhurst. I arrived late in the afternoon, about 5.40 pm. As a black kelpie ran out to greet me, barking loudly, I noticed a bearded bloke in an old hat following. He gave me a wave. Immediately I knew he was a character. His surround's showed a man who was very much an individualist: flag flying, old windmill of sorts turning (or was it a generator?), odd collection of cars, and bits and pieces of all sorts of 'stuff' scattered about – what you'd expect of a bushie in a camp off the beaten path. The place reeked with that 'I'm a bloody bushie, all right?' feeling.

Alf was dressed in shorts, thongs, an open shirt that flapped in the breeze, showing a grey-haired chest with a long beard covering most of it, and a bush hat. Yep, he's a bushie, all right, I thought, and yep, he looks like he might be eccentric. Is there such a look?

'A rough roof with hardly any sides' – at work in the studio.

We shook hands and I told him I'd driven all this way just to see him. He seemed pleased and soon we were into it; two blokes having a yarn, as blokes do. We walked to his studio – a rough roof with hardly any sides to it, junk all around – and beside some small trees, an open-air gallery of his work. There they were: marvellous, unique, intrinsically quizzical sculptures sitting on rough benches raised high off the ground. Inside the studio I saw a small table covered in rough hand tools – obviously this was his work area. Opposite was a small collection of sculptures, postcards and brochures. His 'shop'.

Alf soon got into his tourist routine of explaining how he developed his thoughts on the alphabet and its origins. I was immediately impressed with the simplicity – and clarity – of his thoughts. It was obvious that he was a well-read man who had long studied the histories of the world and its people. He had a broad knowledge of ancient civilisations and was not stuck for words when explaining his theories.

'Tucker money' – Alf's work attracts an international clientele.

'Instrinsically quizzical sculptures' – now just imagine that Lawson piece ...

I was intrigued and sceptical at the same time, but some of what he said had a strong meaning and common sense about it. I cannot begin to describe it here, and don't be surprised if, when you visit him, you come away no clearer yourself. However, I will say one thing: he really gets you questioning and wondering. He is a good teacher because he makes you think. Some will come away saying he is just an eccentric who's been in the sun too long, but usually those who are quick to judge need to look in their own mirrors first.

I am always questioning and have a huge thirst for knowledge. I live by what my grandmother said: she learnt something new every day of her life until she was ninety-five and I try to live that way now.

I told Alf I'd seen him on TV and read bits about him, but I really knew nothing about him and I wanted to, and I was keen to write a story on him if it was OK. Without hesitation, he was happy to oblige.

'Oh, there's a snake,' said Alf, immediately getting to his feet.

I looked around and, sure enough, there beside the wall a few feet away, a long skinny snake about 4 feet long was slowly crawling along. I froze, my leg was crossed and if I moved too quickly I knew this thing would strike. I looked further to my right to see Alf's kelpie asleep close by. Alf was standing now, ready to throw a huge hammer head at the snake, but my leg was in the way; he stood firm as we watched to see what its next movement would be.

It slithered along the wall, its tongue flicking in and out, and all the while getting closer to my leg. I slowly moved my leg and got ready to take an almighty leap backwards.

I was worried, though, that the snake would retreat, and if the dog woke, it would be bitten. Sure enough, the snake turned the minute I moved and the area just behind its head flattened – a sign of aggression. It moved quickly (but, thankfully, not quickly enough) as I leapt back as fast as I could without waking Mr Bojangles, the dog, who stirred and sat up just as the snake darted behind a drum and disappeared. He knew something was amiss and was looking towards where the snake had disappeared. Alf called the dog away, but he was still looking at the snake's retreat and moved to investigate. Alf and I both gingerly checked as well, but luckily it was gone.

Now, that long, skinny bastard really had me worried at the time. I felt it was either me or the dog that was going to get bitten. For the next few minutes as Alf and I resumed our interview, I kept looking back, worried about Mr Bojangles. And besides, no snake was going to sneak up on me again this day, let me tell you that!

We settled back to our chat.

'I was born Cornelis Johan Alferink and emigrated to Australia from Holland in 1953, when I was seven. I arrived in Fremantle, Western Australia, with my parents, Annie and Johan, and a brother and three sisters. My father had been a cavalryman in the Dutch Army in World War II and when we arrived we were sent to the Northern Migrant Camp for a month, before Dad was employed as a farm manager for a local doctor near Margaret River. Five years later we moved onto our own land – a 230-acre bush block opposite the now famous Leeuwin winery. Nowadays, my brother owns the farm. I was at school between '53 and '61, then left to start a job on Maralana Station, south of Marble Bar.'

It would be the start of many wanderings for Alf.

'In 1962 I saw an ad in the paper for a geologist's assistant in the Pilbara region. I got the job in an interview over the phone. I was

'Eureka Stockade, Aborigines, convicts' – even his old ute has a confronting message.

to work for an American exploration company, exploring for iron ore for D. K. Ludwig to build his own ships. For seven or eight years on and off I was a field assistant, doing all types of work in geologist camps, from mechanic assistant to driver on a Trackscavator. Then I was at Goldsworthy, 80 miles east of Nullagine at Mt Rove camp; two years at La Port Exploration Company looking for titanium in their exploration branch; at Bunbury doing field work for beach sand; two or three years looking for copper and tin around Marble Bar. Basically, I was getting paid to travel and look around.'

Naturally, I wanted to know how he first got interested in working with talcum.

'I first saw talc in 1964 between Greenbush and Balingup. I threw some in the back of the Land Rover, and in the Sunday camp, on a day off, I sat and carved a piece with a pocket knife. Some call it soapstone.

'The first major carving I did was an abstract head and hand carving like the famous sculpture *The Thinker*. It now sits in the Margaret River Library. I gave it to them when I'd gone home to see the family. It is on the desk where the librarian sits.

'Mum can remember how when I was about four or five years old I made a sculpture of a rabbit from bread dough – she saw I had an early interest. When I first went to school I still couldn't speak good English and I learnt more by drawing Mickey Mouse and Donald Duck cartoon characters for the other kids.

'In 1969 I was at Orange Creek Station in the centre of Australia, near Alice Springs, as a backhoe driver for Bell Bros building a bitumen road south. I travelled south for Christmas and in 1970 saw my sister in Melbourne, where she was working as a nurse. As I was travelling, I checked out all the talc deposits in

South Australia. I was locked up at Marree one night for resisting arrest for supporting Labor and Gough Whitlam, as well as for opposing the Vietnam War. I took a swing at one of the local constables for unfair arrest. The Justice of the Peace was a local squatter and a Liberal, as was the publican. I also checked out the talc deposits near Lyndhurst then.

'Once back south, I took the Land Rover and caravan up north over the Sydney Harbour Bridge to Queensland and got a job in a sugar cane factory. For a while I was then back at the caravan park in Gawler, South Australia, where I carved Lyndhurst talc. Then to Myrtleford in Victoria, picking tobacco for some Italians on a farm for about three months, before heading to Queensland again, to Cairns and the Atherton Tablelands, chasing talc from deposits between Mareeba and Atherton, but also working on a cement-laying gang doing culverts near Cairns. In 1972 I was making money by carving talc and selling sculptures at the flea market in Cairns.

'I lived at Kuranda, which was great. I ran into a Thursday Island lady called Daisy in Cairns. She had been a cook at the Grand Hotel and we made our home in Kuranda. Talc ran low and for about six months I was at Innisfail. Then we went back south again.

'Daisy went home to Thursday Island and a mate of mine asked me to go on his yacht with him on the round-the-world trip. It was a hard decision, to sell up or go with him. Anyway, to cut a long story short, I ended up in Brisbane as a backhoe driver on a sewerage site for about four months, and still no letter from Daisy, so I decided to head back to South Australia. I was about to leave when a letter arrived. She flew down to Brisbane and we came back here. When we came south in 1974 we went to Leigh

Creek and got married, and in January 1975 our daughter Diat was born. She's now in Port Adelaide as director of Kururu Youth Theatre, teaching 110 kids.

'Basically, my travels have been about chasing one talc deposit after another.

'When we came to Lyndhust in 1974, we arrived on Good Friday and camped on the common just out of town; we parked the caravan on top of this sandhill, threw out the annex and have been here ever since. I've never had a government handout in my life, and I got a job here one day a week in a truckie workshop while I carved talc, which I then sold through the shop to tourists. Later I got a job for the talc mine, shovelling 20 ton of talc from a flat-top truck onto a railway truck, just me and Bill Clark. A tough job. Then I worked for two contractors loading 40 ton with a tipper and front-end loader for about twenty years. The boss gave me the OK to collect as much talc as I needed for my carvings, then the railway closed in the early 1980s, so I really got stuck into carvings and sold through the shop. Since 1974, on average I've been making at least one carving a day over thirty-one years. Some days, might be one, but other days up to six. The small head shapes sell for $10 on average, so one a day is tucker money for the day.

'It's a bit of a struggle for Daisy here in summer, so sometimes she takes a few carvings to Adelaide to sell through art shops. She stays with our daughter and mainly spends winter up here. I sell a lot of head-shaped sculptures and all sorts of abstract ones. Many tourist coaches come here, mainly backpackers touring the outback.'

There's no doubt that Talc Alf is famous; people overseas know him before they arrive and many Australians have heard of him.

'A great Australian bush character' – a sketch of Talc Alf.

He has featured in many television shows and all sorts of print media. People who travel the outback in four-wheel drives usually do the Strzelecki Track, and Talc Alf is here at the start of the southern end. He is one of those great Aussie bush characters. He has lived as he wants and now the rough-hewn home he built himself stands beside the outdoor gallery of his works. He has stamped his character on this part of the world and without him Lyndhurst would not be as well known.

We got on like two bush mates do and I appreciated many of his comments on life, the bush and more. And besides, he likes Henry Lawson, so he must be a good bloke. I read some of Alf's rough notes detailing his theories on the alphabet, which I can't claim to have understood, but some of it was very clear and I agreed with it. You need to visit him and make up your own mind. I take people as I find them and I found him very obliging, friendly, caring and generous. So much so we talked long into the evening and I didn't leave until nearly 10 pm. Meeting him was well worth the drive.

'A quick side trip' – a sign for the Strzelecki Track.

Now I had four of his carvings to take pride of place on my wall. Talc Alf gave me one to join the carving given by Joe Daley, plus I bought two. And I'd have to leave room for a special Henry Lawson one as well. I would await its completion with anticipation – yet another piece to add to my large and growing collection of Lawson items.

The following morning I drove back to see Alf and take some photos. He showed me the old Holden ute that he drove across the Nullarbor, painted up with a copy of his own flag and such. It was now well and truly dying from rust rigor mortis.

It was time for us both to hit the road, he to commence his other job as the local mailman (yet another entry on his CV), me to head home. His new Land Rover was packed and ready to head bush along the lonely tracks of this part of South Australia, where a rugged beauty is always there for those who take time to look.

But this story would not be complete without a final word from Talc Alf himself. Leaving aside his carvings of the alphabet, I ask him, how does he sum up his pictorial carvings and what they say? Why do so many have historical themes, like the Eureka Stockade, Burke and Wills, Aborigines, convicts, Simpson and his donkey, and more?

'I want to do something useful for Australia and pass on knowledge,' he replies. 'It's to record the history of Australia – it's communication through the arts.'

Before we head south again and on to our next outbacker, let's go off on what I term the 'Nowhere Track'. I've decided to take a quick side trip along one of the tracks just for something to do

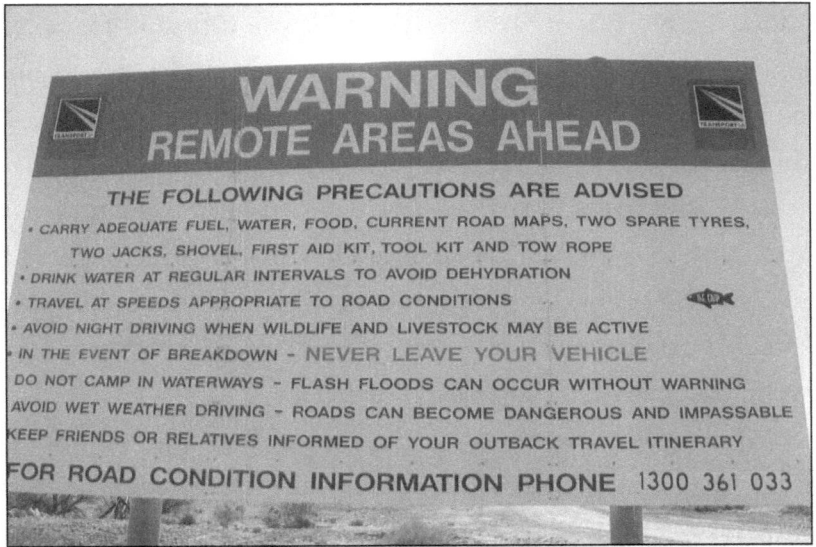

They like to keep an eye on things out here

and see. I'd really like to 'do' part of the Strzelecki, Birdsville or Oodnadatta tracks right here and now, but don't have time, so you'll have to put up with some more dirt while I detour for a bit, then we'll get back onto the real trip.

You see, sometimes I just need to go somewhere on a map and it doesn't have to be for a reason. I have a continual urge, and when travelling I may decide I want to see the ocean or the mountains, or it might simply be to spend time in an isolated spot and see the sun go down on my own. I may want to take a photo or write about something, or just take in the environment. The outback, particularly, can do that to me. I can remember once being hundreds of miles into the outback and had a real urge to see the ocean; so I drove for the next three days … and ended up at Byron Bay! Being a writer on the move can take you on some long trips.

THE NOWHERE TRACK

I love the Sturt Stony Desert. Out here, you can walk for miles and see nothing but stones – deep red stones, all the way to the horizon. It make you feel like a speck, insignificant and alone. I find that absolutely amazing and attractive.

It doesn't matter where we are now – I'm not going to tell you. You have to imagine it. It is isolated, only a rough old roadhouse, a couple of rundown shacks that match the roadhouse, some Aboriginal kids, a few tourists in four-wheel drives. And we've just arrived, to buy a few supplies.

We are many miles from anywhere in any direction. Soon we'll head back to our main route again, across lonely lands. Let me introduce you to 'Blue', one of the many brief encounters you always have in the outback.

'G'day mate,' he says to me. 'Nice ute.'

'Thanks.'

'So, where you headed?'

His gut is bigger than mine and hangs low over his baggy shorts. He's munching on an ice-cream bought in the old roadhouse, where we've all stopped for a breather from the dusty road. He attacks the ice-cream as it melts in the heat. He hasn't seen that his T-shirt already has a brown bird-shit-like stain of brown chocolate down the front.

'The Nowhere Track,' I reply as I walk towards him and my ute.

'What's that thing on the roof of your ute?'

'That's a Sat-Trak two-way satellite system.'

'That like a GPS thing, is it?'

'Yeah, but much more. I can receive and send messages and such.'

'Mmm, flash,' he says as he devours the rest of the ice-cream.

I unload the few supplies I've bought onto the front seat of my ute. It is hot, dry and out in the middle of nowhere. The roadhouse is the only lifeline for travellers for many hundreds of miles around this part of the outback.

As I turn to face him, his number 6 vice grabs me. I know it's a vice because no hand can grip that tight. I look him in the eye and grow weaker as my bones slowly turn to dust. Is that smile on his face genuine friendliness or is he just enjoying my pain? The blood slowly starts to return when he lets go of my hand.

'Name's Blue,' he says.

Of course it is, I think. What else would it be, with your red hair and sunburnt freckles on your shoulders, arms and face? But your hair is going grey, too, you old bastard. (Why is it we often call red-haired blokes 'Bluey'? Red, I can understand.)

'Allan,' I reply, 'but most people just call me The Uteman.'

'Nice ta meet ya, young fella. Yeah, nice bloody ute all right.'

This bloke is a questions man. I can tell, as he looks the ute over, there'll be a lot of questions and we'll be here a bit longer. My ute always gets a lot of attention – it's a great conversation starter and I meet a lot of people as a result.

'What track did you say you were going on?' he asks.

'The Nowhere Track.'

He looks at me. 'Where the fuck is the Nowhere Track?'

He has a look that says, *Shit, I haven't seen that on my maps, I must have missed it.* People travelling the outback hate to think they've missed something.

'I'm always on the Nowhere Track – heading everywhere, but always changing my mind and direction, so I call it the Nowhere Track. Nowhere in particular, but everywhere is a possibility and somewhere is the destination.'

He eyes me in silence, still not sure if I'm taking the piss out of him.

'I've changed direction,' I continue, 'but now I think I'm heading southwest towards Adelaide. Who knows.'

'Ah right,' he smiles. 'You had me wondering for a bit there. I was just going to ask the missus for a map so you could show me how to get there.' He's laughing now.

The 'missus' is eating an ice-cream close to where her husband has parked their Toyota Land Crusier and caravan, near the only tree in sight. The missus looks bored.

'We're doing "the big lap". You know, driving around Australia.' He looks towards the Toyota and caravan with a quiet sense of pride. It's a nice set-up. Big and flash. The caravan is big, all right – real big. Then a touch of regret creeps into his voice. 'Mum misses the kids and the grandkids, so we're heading home now.' He pauses.

Blue's hand seems to have turned my hand into a throbber. It's instantly obvious to me that he is a working man. Big firm handshake, with rough hands. His whole demeanour spells 'worker'.

'So, you retired, Blue?'

'Yeah, sort of. We got a couple of fruit blocks on the Murray near Mildura in Victoria. I took over me dad's place as well. Now, though, my two boys pretty well run the show and reckon I'm in the way, so the missus and I decided to take twelve months off and see Australia. This is our first trip away anywhere really. Bloody great place, isn't it?'

Blue is one of those blokes you meet who you spend minutes yacking with and you get his life story. And he's happy to yarn for as long as you want.

'So, how long you been on the road then?' I ask.

'A bit over five months or so.' He kicks my front tyre and looks around the ute more. I wonder why men like to kick tyres.

'So, you headed home now, you say?'

'Yeah, we'll be home in about six weeks. A lot sooner than I'd like, but you know what women are like. "Mum" is OK in her kitchen but the caravan ain't like home for her. She doesn't like caravanning much.'

'Looks like a nice van.'

'Ah, yeah, shit, she's got everything – 26-footer, every bloody mod con. Satellite TV, air-conditioning, shower and toilet, washing machine – all the stuff she wanted but still not enough.'

'You like to travel then?'

'Oh, shit yeah. I could do this for the rest of my life. Fishing, seeing things, drinking a stubbie with people you meet in caravan parks or in the bush. Seeing the country. Geez, this is a great country, isn't it?'

He is a man of statements as well as questions.

We swap our stories for nearly twenty-five minutes and talk of places, vehicles and even the price of petrol. 'Road talk', I call it.

'What a job you've got then, getting paid to travel Australia. Half ya luck, mate.'

'Yeah, I love it,' I say. 'It has its downs too, though.'

'God, what?' he asks.

'Gets a bit lonely at times as well. I miss the wife and my dog. It's always good to get home.' He nods. 'But after about a week or so I think, Wonder what it's like in some out-of-the-way place … And so off I go to find out.'

'Mate, you got the best of both worlds,' he says.

'Yeah, suppose I have.'

We shake hands again, but it doesn't matter – he's already killed it. And off he goes.

As the dust rises from his vehicle and caravan, his wife gives me a feeble wave and a smile. He toots his horn and they are gone. I stand there watching them disappear down the dirt road towards the turnoff to Charleville.

Blue probably doesn't realise how lucky he is. Wife, kids and grandkids. Family. I wish my wife was with me now. And I miss my dog. Sometimes the Nowhere Track can be the Lonely Track.

I'm still a couple of thousand miles from home.

That's what it's like out here. You meet many of the Blues of this world. He'll probably never travel much again. He's done the 'big trip' of his life; he won't get his wife on the road again. And so life will go on and he'll see his grandkids grow. There are many stories of lives on the roads of Australia. I get to share in many of them.

For me, too, it's time to hit the road, and the noise of the V8 rumbles in my ear. The sun beats down and I head towards the end of another day, out where the trees dance on the shimmering haze in the distance.

It really is a great country.

We arrive back at Lyndhurst. We'll be back on track as soon as I fill up the ute with petrol. A lady I meet as I fill the tank is the daughter of a great Birdsville drover and we yarn for a while. We've met before. She's not usually very impressed with tourists. She's seen some of the stupid things they do and impose on the locals. Stupid questions usually get a gruff answer. Soon it's time to leave. We bid farewell and I tell her I'll see her again on the next trip. She smiles and waves me goodbye. An overnight camp next to the pub at Lyndhurst, a pub feed, a yarn – and a long sleep.

After an early start, it's a straight run south from Lyndhurst towards Hawker to an interview I've wanted to do but never got around to. But, as usual, my plan doesn't run true to form.

From Leigh Creek we head on past Beltana and arrive at Parachilna, and here I decide to do a bit more sidetracking. Just for the hell of it.

BLINMAN

I arrive at Blinman, an isolated settlement on the edge of the South Australian desert, 485 kilometres north of Adelaide via Wilpena Pound. Population: 20. One of Blinman's claims to fame

'Population: 20' – the highest town in South Australia.

is that it's the highest town in South Australia, although Amata, in the state's far northwest, also claims that honour.

Copper was discovered at Blinman by a wooden-legged shepherd, Robert 'Peg Leg' Blinman, in 1859. Copper was mined in the area from around 1862 through to 1918, when the ore ran out. On the hill above the town there are remains of old smelters and other bits and pieces. All are remnants of the late nineteenth century when the town was alive with miners.

One of the main attractions is the Blinman Cemetery, which lies at the southern end of the town. Here are graves of men killed working with explosives near the mine, and of William Kekwick (died 1872), who was the second-in-charge to John McDouall Stuart when he crossed Central Australia.

It's now beer o'clock, so I decided to have a cooked lunch at the pub and a yarn to the owner. He tells me to make sure to come back when they have the next camp-oven cookout – great cooks compete using just camp ovens. Next to the pub are the remains of many camp fires. I must add the cookout to my list of things to do; I'll come back for the right tucker at the right time.

After a nice lunch it's time to head for Wilpena Pound, 59 kilometres to the south via the heart of the Flinders Ranges. I've been there before and flown over it, but this time I want to get a photo of a tree.

THE CAZNEAUX TREE

Aussie adventurer and successful businessman Dick Smith has a special interest in the tree I've come to photograph, a few kilometres north of the Wilpena tourist development. His

'Special interest' – no problem finding this particular tree!

'A true love of Australia' – the memorial to Dick Smith's grandfather.

'Leafy boughs' – the author's own 'Spirit of Endurance'.

grandfather, Harold Cazneaux, who won many Australian and international photographic awards, photographed this tree in 1937. He named the photo 'The Spirit of Endurance' and said he stood before it 'in silent wonder and admiration. The hot wind stirred its leafy boughs and some of the living element of this tree passed to me in understanding and friendliness expressing The Spirit of Australia.'

His grandson certainly seems to have inherited a true love of Australia. A memorial was donated and unveiled by Dick Smith, then publisher of *Australian Geographic* magazine, in 1991. As a great lover of trees (I photograph them all over Australia), I have to add this old eucalypt to my collection.

Soon, I was ready to head south. There was no time to overnight at Wilpena. I could spend more time telling you all about the place, but I have a bloke I want you to meet, so it's off to Arkaba.

But not tonight, I just want for another night in the swag under the Southern Cross, enjoying the bush and the outback skies. The peace, the smells, the brisk night air and afterall, this is what the outback is all about; getting back close to nature, memories of the explorers and the pioneers. Alone with one's own thoughts. Soon, in a quiet out of the way spot I am laying in the swag looking at the wonders of the night sky before sleep finally overtakes me.

'Greets anyone with a smile' – Gordon Coulthard, horse lover.

ARKABA

GORDON COULTHARD, ONE OF THE ROCK PEOPLE

'Spiritually, it's very pleasing being on this land.
Plenty bush tucker. I like Chinese tucker too though.'

I met him in Hawker initially, but his story is to the north, at Arkaba, on the track towards Wilpena.

I am off the main road and under the shade of a huge gum tree. It is quiet, no cars, no one around and only magpies break the silence. Magpies provide travellers like me with a warm feeling; I always feel like they are talking to me. They also remind me of the ones we hand-fed at home, Arthur and Martha and their kids. The story that follows is of a traditional owner of country north of Hawker, in the southern Flinders Ranges. Part of his spirit country is near where he has a caravan and horses –

where he regains his spiritual feelings when he's away from the big smoke of Port Augusta.

I was seated under a shop verandah in Hawker, having a morning drink and a sandwich and reading the *Adelaide Advertiser*, when an Aboriginal man walked towards his old ute parked in the gutter next to me, a panting kelpie dog tied up in the back.

'G'day brother,' he said with a smile. Gordon has no worries making conversation with strangers. He greets anyone with a smile and is only too happy to have a yarn. We swapped small talk about last night's heavy rain and the flooding creeks, then he sat down and settled in for a good yarn. He wanted to talk about the Melbourne Cup.

'I've seen Makybe Diva win three times at the cup,' he told me. He also remembered Empire Rose, who won in 1988. 'She was a big mare. I also saw Ethereal win in the rain with Scott Seamer on board. I got on a plane in Adelaide at 6.45 am and when I got

Gordon and a couple of his horses, Arkaba Station.

to Melbourne, I shared a taxi and went straight to Flemington and was there by 9 am. It's a good day at Flemington.'

Gordon was keen to know if Harry Down still made saddles. He had a couple but wanted some new ones. I agreed to find out and let him know. I assumed Gordon was a horse lover. He mentioned that he had ten horses now out on Arkaba Station.

We talked some more and it was his friendly nature and openness to a stranger that made me want to know more of this man. We agreed I should follow him in his ute and go look at his horses.

We got set to leave as a young tourist couple sat down at another table. 'G'day, how you going?' said Gordon with a smile. They responded and said they were going to Wilpena.

'You just arrived, have you?'

They confirmed that they had.

'We are going out to show him my horses,' Gordon said, as an open invitation to the couple. 'Arkaba Woolshed – you'll see it on the side of the road and my horses in the paddock.'

With that, we left them to their morning tea.

A short time later and we were at the gates of Arkaba Station Woolshed, a historic stone shed built in 1856 and still in use. Gordon doesn't live at Arkaba, but he comes here every now and then from his home in Port Augusta ('the Crossroads of Australia') to spend time in the bush.

As before, we check out the horses, in a corral, four quiet ones, including Cathy Freeman ('cause she's a bit of a runner, this one'). We then make our way past the shearing shed to Gordon's caravan, beside some trees and a small corral, where another horse is kept. That one got kicked in the nose by another horse, so he's here for a while. The kelpie, Rob, is taken off the ute and tied up in the shade of a horse float. Gordon gets a couple of glasses of fruit juice from inside his caravan and we settle underneath the shade, overlooking his camp; in the background is the magnificent scenery of the ranges. Here we talk of all sorts of things, and Gordon is very happy to tell me more of his life.

'I was born on Neppabunna in about 1934 or 1935, I think it was. It's about 60 kilometres east of Leigh Creek, an Aboriginal reserve. I think it was UAM – United Aboriginal Mission or something like that.' He sips his cool drink and looks across his land. 'My mother was Annie Mckenzie, born about 1905 on Wooltana Station, and my father was Sam Coulthard, a boundary rider on Wooltana. My family included three sisters and four brothers. Doreen (deceased) was the eldest, then Jim (he's at Quorn), then me, Leo (deceased), Arthur (deceased); Margaret is at Quorn and Sarah at Port Augusta.

'How we became Coulthards is, I believe, an old Scotsman called Coulthard many years ago jumped ship and ended up making his way up here and became friendly with the Aboriginals. And that's how it all started. David Coulthard, the race driver, he's one of them from over there.'

Gordon gets the pen and paper off me to write down his family tribal name: Adnyamathanha. 'That's who we are.' He repeats it, trying to show me how to say it properly. 'It means we are the Rock People,' he says proudly, but in a matter-of-fact way.

'I went to school on Neppabunna for a couple of years, and then I was put on a horse at about thirteen years old. And that was it, my first job – riding a grey horse on Wooltana – riding the fence during shearing, checking fences, rounding up sheep.

'Afterwards I went doing contract work: yard building, fencing, shearing. I worked all over – down at Yunta, Cockburn and way up into Queensland, near Quilpie and Windorah mainly. Cattle droving for many miles. Down the Diamantina. You see, they used to get cattle ready for the Christmas market, and we'd drove them down south to fatten them up; they were for store cattle. Later they would get shipped off by rail.

'I was also involved a lot with cattle on Frome Downs Station, northeast of Wilpena.

'You know, in the old days it was hard. They'd drove cattle for fifteen weeks with about thirty to forty horses and work from 4 am until 10 pm at night. The horses had no chaff or hay; they just fed off the green feed of the land. They were tough.

'You can only work cattle early morning and late afternoon or early evening. I drove six weeks from Cordillo Downs to Quilpie, and then the cattle were loaded onto trains for the market in Brisbane.

'I drove from the top end of Lake Frome, near the New South Wales border fence, down to Cockburn, and there were two train-loads of cattle to ship off. We did two trips a year. I worked from 1953 to 1964 or thereabouts doing that. In between droving trips, I did fencing work. I was never without a job.

'Then, about 1967, I was doing windmill work – building them and drilling bores. I worked with many drilling rigs, looking for water. About 1967 I built a vermin-proof netting fence on Indulkana Aboriginal Reserve, south of the Northern Territory border.

'In 1969 to 1970 I worked at ETSA Powerhouse in Port Augusta for two-and-a-half years, as an assistant to the boilermakers and fitter and turners. After that I joined the

Commonwealth Railways at the Port Augusta workshops as an office assistance and stayed there ten years.'

Gordon found working in an office suited him, and he would do much more of it.

'Then, well, I sort of got shanghied by the Port Augusta City Council as an Aboriginal liaison officer. And then for ten years I was community reconciliation officer for the Department of Aboriginal Affairs [ATSIC] until 1996, working with mining companies and other interests. It was good. We changed them and they changed us.

'But I had enough of all that, and in late 1997 I took Dean Rasheed from Wilpena Pound horse riding and we became friends. He helped give me the chance to become tour operator on his Arkaba Station here, and with a mate of mine, Rex Stuart, we started to build yards. He got killed in a car accident up north, poor Rex.'

I've visited the memorial to Rex Stuart, deeper into the ranges. The inscription reads:

'This plaque celebrates the life of Rex Stuart, a traditional custodian of the Arabunna people and a true modern-day cowboy. Born in Finniss Springs Station on 13 March 1941, Rex tragically passed away on this hill on the morning of 28 September 2001. Rex was a strong advocate for the protection of Aboriginal heritage and the handing down of traditional knowledge to his children, and was fluent in six Aboriginal languages, and was recognised as one of South Australia's finest Aboriginal language interpreters. One of the great legendary Aboriginal drovers and stockmen, Rex drove stock along the Georgina River, the Caley Cooper Run, and worked as a stockman on Lake Nash Station among others. His passing is sorely lamented. Rex is survived by his wife Angelina and their children Dawn, Nobelene, Aaron, Virginia and Corrina.'

'*A true modern-day stockman*' – the Rex Stuart Memorial.

Ngarabunna (Sturt's desert pea) is the cultural totem of Rex's homeland. (As Gordon has never visited the spot and seen Rex's plaque, I will take photos to show him next time we meet for a yarn.)

'I got a hand in my own land,' he continues. 'I'd be mad to go away from my homeland territory – the Flinders Ranges.

'This land has been a station since 1856. The last Aboriginal to occupy it would have been about 1850, but the land is still good. I like it. Spiritually, it's very pleasing being on this land.'

Gordon points out a tree that in a few months will have fruit, the oil from which, when crushed, tastes like peanut butter. 'Plenty bush tucker. I like Chinese tucker too, though,' he adds with a laugh.

While this is his spiritual home, Gordon has a home in Port Augusta with wife Dawn and daughter Margaret. 'Someone got to look after the house when I'm away,' he says. 'I got to look after my horses.

'Tastes like peanut butter' – Gordon and the tucker tree.

'I've ridden horses in the Colorado Rockies too, you know. In 1990 I won an Aboriginal overseas-study award and spent a month trail riding and studying how to set up a tourism business. I also did tourism on farms in Wisconsin, and went onto a Chippewa Indian reservation.

'Now I'm still involved with cross-cultural workshops – working with big mining bosses, employees, to make them understand our different culture. It goes for both sides, though. I like to be able to do something, not entirely retire, keep it all going for a future role.

'This job is the best one of all I've done, working here with my horses. I'm trying to get young Aboriginals to work for the future – you got to pass it on.

'I keep telling them, "You got to do it, you do it." Sometimes you want to give it away, but one day you will be successful with everything; you just got to keep on doing it. Just keep on doing it.'

Wise words. Gordon and I speak for a while longer of the spirit of this country. He explains what the ranges behind mean for his people. 'Secret men's business there,' he says, pointing to some ridges and creek beds. 'No women go there – they know.' We even discuss Kaidaitcha Man, but out of respect for Gordon and his culture, I won't include anything about him here.

There will be much more to talk about at our next meeting, when he will show me more of these places, and we'll explore by four-wheel drive and on horseback. I look forward to it, to learning more from an old man of the land, a man in tune with his country.

I hope his Arkaba Horse Trails business grows and he stays happy. He has much to teach the young ones. He is at home in the saddle; even in his seventies he is still happy on horseback.

'A picturesque spot' – the dry creek bed lined with beautiful trees.

I'm glad to have shared some time with this friendly, open-hearted man. I ask him one more question. He's come a long way since the days on Neppabunna – what does his life look like? What does it all mean to him now in his older years? He sums it up nicely.

'I don't think I should be whingeing,' he replies. 'I got horses, I got a house, I got two caravans. I got freedom. I go anywhere, with no restriction. I don't drink or smoke.'

And finally he says, with a big smile and a laugh, 'If I can go to the Melbourne Cup every year I'll be happy.'

We shake hands and I get ready to leave. Gordon and I had shared a great yarn together sitting underneath a tree and looking across at the deep blue ranges nearby, beside a dry creek bed lined with beautiful gum trees. A picturesque spot. I look forward to catching up with him again.

'An outback legend' – Fred Teague (1912–1994).

HAWKER TO THE FLINDERS RANGES

FRED TEAGUE, MR FLINDERS RANGES

'Scientists, anthropologists, palaentologists, geologists, naturalists, historians, authors, theologians, photographers, artists – all came to him to share knowledge when researching the area.'

Hawker has long been a stopping point for anyone heading to the Flinders Ranges, particularly to Wilpena Pound. Here I will introduce you to an outback legend. Though he passed away some time ago, we have much information on him; there's even a museum dedicated mainly to his life at the business his son now carries on.

'Proud of Dad' – the Teague family today at Hawker Motors.

They still talk of the hearty pioneers of the Birdsville and Strzelecki tracks as legends. Fred Teague was one of them. He was a mailman in some of the nation's remotest country, when few ventured 'outback'. And today they still talk of Fred Teague years after he's gone to rest.

Unfortunately, I never met him. I reckon we would have had a lot to talk about, but the next best thing is Fred's son John, his wife Janet and their children. It was obvious when I showed interest in Fred's story that the family were proud of 'Dad' and only too happy to assist. I'd read bits and pieces about Fred over the years, but could never find a book on him.

That is the first question I ask when I walk into Hawker Motors, the business Fred started in the 1950s, late on a Friday afternoon. John Teague worked for his dad from the age of sixteen; then, when he married, the three of them worked in partnership. Now the business is run by John and his wife Janet and their son. Their daughter helps out too.

'Dad was mentioned in about forty books over the years, just short pieces,' says John, while photocopying some stuff for me.

'There should be a book written about him, I reckon,' I offer, adding quickly that unfortunately I can't take on any more projects.

I decide to interview John the next morning, so for now I go off to a local caravan park to sleep. It rained heavily all night. The roads are in flood, but the rains, long overdue, are welcomed by the locals.

I head back to Hawker Motors, where I fill up with fuel a little after 7.30 am. By 7.40 am, John and I are sitting at a table discussing his family's history, with the emphasis on his father.

'Often people come into the business with yarns of what they remember about Dad,' John begins.

Fred Teague was a legend in his own lifetime, not just after he died. He was a man who worked hard and learnt and shared. They don't call you 'Mr Flinders Ranges' for doing nothing with your life.

He was born in Olary, South Australia, in 1912, three months after his father died. He was raised primarily by his sister because his mother had to work very hard to ensure that her young family survived. When she became a widow, his mother had an eight-year-old daughter, two younger sons, and Fred, the new baby. As he lay dying, Fred's father told his wife that she should marry his mate Paddy, who would look after her and the children. In time, that's exactly what happened.

As a lad, Fred helped his mother in her Waukaringa Hotel, and went out to work while still young. On one occasion he was left out in a camp by himself with two weeks' worth of rations – flour, water, jam, dripping and salt meat. The water was rationed at just a quart a day.

On another occasion, alone in the bush again, he developed a tooth abscess and his face became badly swollen. Realising his isolation from medical aid, he had no choice but to suck the pus out of the tooth. He thought his head would lift off, the pain in the nerves was so dreadful. His clear thinking, however, saved him from becoming very sick or even dying.

Time rolls on at Hawker Motors and by 9 am it's starting to get pretty busy, with a constant flow of people paying for fuel, buying stores and having a yak to the staff. I'm grateful for John's time in this busy part of the day.

'Dad later became a gold prospector, fox shooter, drover and he worked in the droving camps as a horsetailer when he was only fourteen. (The lowest job in camp: he had to get up earlier than anyone else to fetch the horses, and was last into the swag at night as he had to hobble the horses.) He also worked in shearing sheds, and drove trucks.'

Fred became a truck driver and worked for the legendary H.E. (Harry) Ding, another pioneer of the Birdsville Track. Driving for Harry Ding involved transporting prized rams as well as general cargo. Fred then took on the mail run up the Birdsville Track for Ding. It was while he was doing the mail that he first became interested in collecting things – stones, Aboriginal artefacts, old bottles and other collectables. He drove the mail before even the pedal radio and long before there was a road of any kind. It was a *real* track and was prone to all sorts of changes due to the elements (sand drifts, mud and such). He had to do his own repairs and manufacture spare parts. He carted all the materials used for the hospital at Innamincka.

Fred met his wife Eileen in 1937 in Lyndhurst, where she lived. He was driving the Marree–Birdsville Mail at the time. They were

'A man who worked hard and shared' – Fred (second from right) and fellow gold prospectors.

'Pioneer of the Birdsville Track' – driving for H.E. Ding.

'Dedicated service to the community' – hard yakka in the outback.

married in Peterborough in 1940. The couple had five children: Carlene, Marjorie, John, Cheryl and Sharon. They moved to Hawker on Australia Day, 1941. He then drove the Carrieton Mail from 1941 for Harry Ding until he bought the run himself.

In 1952 Fred bought A.T. Edwards & Sons General Store and worked at nights to transform the shop into a garage while he continued to drive the mail during the day. Hawker Motors opened later the same year. In those early days he sold fridges, cars and tractors, and became the first South Australian Gas Co agent. He also sold TVs when they became available.

It was all this early travelling work that made Fred see the potential for tourism, and he encouraged locals to build accommodation for tourists. He became a driving force behind the tourist industry in the Flinders, forming the first Flinders Tourism Committee. He ended up getting many awards over the years – two from the Flinders Ranges Regional Tourist Association alone – in recognition of his dedicated service to tourism and the community in general. He even got a posthumous one.

Fred could see that travellers needed car services and information about the area, as well as good roads, accommodation – and no gates. He was instrumental in having gates removed from the main roads (grids are now used instead). He also saw the need to ensure that Aboriginal sites were protected.

He and Eileen were both extremely generous. 'Dad was always bringing someone home for a meal, often a complete stranger, a passing traveller, someone whose car broke down, or someone from the bush just passing through.'

There was always a meal for anyone at the Teague table. John's family remembers many a swag rolled out on the lounge-room floor; later, the Teagues had a caravan they never got to use because of the travellers who were put up in it. Many, many people remember the generosity of the Teague family, with Mrs Teague cooking steak and eggs late at night to fill an empty belly. As if this were not enough, the Teagues also looked after Eileen's mother, who was blind, deaf and unable to walk.

In 1986 the original garage closed and the Teagues moved across the road into their current premises.

Fred was an inventor too. One day, a traveller pulled into Fred's garage, his car's engine making a terrible racket. There was some difference in opinion as to the cause of the noise, and soon Fred brought out his 'Phonoscope' to see what the problem was. This homemade apparatus consisted of the earpiece of an old telephone handset with a piece of brass welding rod poked through the centre. The secret of its success was, apparently (as explained by John, quoting his father), 'the flexible mounting of the earpiece and the close tolerance in locating the end of the bass rod – just touch the metal diaphragm'. (This was Fred's tongue-in-cheek way of saying, 'I'm the mechanic; leave me alone.') Using this device, Fred could listen to problems inside the engine. He'd made it just after the war and had been using it ever since. The problem was soon fixed and the traveller, a man with twenty-five years' experience as an acoustics engineer, had just met a man who didn't need a university degree.

Fred went on to become a fellow of the Royal Society of South Australia, a justice of the peace, local coroner and a member of the Freemasons. He served on many boards and committees, including the school council and the rodeo and camera clubs. He showed pictures at the local institute for many years and ran the town powerhouse for a time. He even had a role as an extra in the *Boney* television series. All this and he still ran his own garage

'A driving force behind the tourist industry' – Fred's garage, a local landmark since 1952.

'People from all walks of life' – Fred at work, serving a motorist.

'Travellers needed car services' – and still do; Hawker Motors today.

business and, for almost forty years, was the RAA contractor, a role John fills now.

'Dad was extremely well known and many people from all over the world met or corresponded with him. He met people from many walks of life – scientists, anthropologists, naturalists, historians, authors, theologians, photographers, artists. All came to him to share knowledge when researching the area.'

People like Charles Mountford, the anthropologist; Len Beadell, surveyor of many outback tracks; Dick Smith, explorer and entrepreneur; Sir Douglas Mawson, the Antarctic explorer; Sir Mark Oliphant, governor and scientist; and artist Sir Hans Heysen.

He had a deep interest in the Flinders, particularly anything to do with geology, archaeology and anthropology. Aboriginal elders regarded Fred as a trusted friend, someone they were willing to share their knowledge with on trips into the bush. In return, Fred understood and respected their knowledge.

Fred is remembered as having a very good eye for the bush. He would see things long before anyone else, and was very much in tune with the environment. He would look at a piece of land and somehow know where to find ancient relics from Aboriginal campfires or interesting geological pieces.

He lived a full life and had many interests. He kept bees. He grew fruit trees of all sorts and grapes of many varieties. He experimented with grafting. He grew vegetables. He tumbled stones for his collection. He was an avid reader and had a great memory for details and facts. He loved Australiana, poems, books of ballads and history. He loved maps and was always studying books on the things he collected – shells, gems, old bottles, old books, coins and stamps – and Aboriginal history, culture and customs.

'Wonderful ambassador' – John Teague, continuing his father's good work.

Fred Teague worked in the garage right up until his death on 11 March 1994, aged eighty-one.

John Donnellan, a friend, spoke at Fred's memorial service: 'Fred was an unforgettable character, equally at ease with scientific professors and all types of professional people as he was with bushmen, truckies and all the rest of the ordinary people, and that included children. He was a kind, patient, tolerant and friendly person, full of wisdom and knowledge, and possessed a great sense of humour. He was well known beyond the borders of South Australia; in fact when travelling interstate, when you mention Hawker, the immediate question would be "How's Fred Teague?" Not only has Hawker lost an outstanding citizen, but South Australia has been deprived of a wonderful ambassador.'

Another who spoke was the Rev. Merv Norman, who said of Fred: 'I marvelled at his bushcraft, and what he was able to see in trees and creeks where I saw nothing, until with great care and infinite patience, he would explain the mystery and point out what must be obvious to any reasonable being.

'I envied his ability to relate to people across cultures. He accepted people as they were. To my knowledge, Aboriginal people as well as the white community regarded him with great affection and respect. From time to time, all were equally welcome in his home. Despite limited formal education, he rose well above any limitation this imposed upon him. I feel my most apt description of this intelligent, multi-talented man would be a quiet, gentle, generous man, with a wonderful patience and a great sense of humour. It always seemed to me that Fred was a man who lived to serve.'

Pretty good sort of memories of this great man. He will not be forgotten. John was always very close to his father. Fred's memory is in good hands with John, and the rest of the family. The museum Fred started – with his collection of objects found on his travels – is still here. I've told John he needs to make the museum bigger and, as he owns a house across the road, I hope if I pester him enough he'll eventually get around to doing so. I look forward to seeing it. After all, people will be talking about not only Fred in years to come but John as well.

It's time for me to head further off, but not before John explains the machine I've spotted in the corner. It is a

'A very good eye for the bush' – Fred surveys his domain.

seismograph installed by the South Australian Primary Industries and Resources Department. John keeps daily records on earthquake activity in the area. The seismograph is the recording equipment that stores the signal of the earth's movement, and Hawker gets a lot of activity. The Teagues continue to assist in gaining knowledge that Fred would have felt important.

I doubt there will ever be another 'Mr Flinders Ranges', but John certainly is carrying on the family tradition and many outback travellers know him well. I'm glad I spent some time with him and shall return yet again for a yarn.

I come away with many pages of notes, together with clippings and photos provided by John. I do a photo shoot with all the family and with John by himself. Then it's handshakes and a promise of 'You'll hear from me again' and I leave them to it.

I decide to go have a look at the Panorama Gallery diagonally opposite and buy a few pieces of art for my wife. She likes anything to do with kookaburras. Then I go to the shop to get a paper because my wife has rung to tell me to buy the *Advertiser*. Her aunt in Adelaide had called her to say that there's an article about what I've done as an outback ambassador, so she thinks I'd better take a copy home for her to read. Janette's a South Australian, but I've converted her to a Victorian.

Time for a malted milk, a sandwich and a read of the paper underneath the shop verandah. Soon after, I head out of town.

HEADING TOWARDS HOME

I wander through tracks east again – as before, getting off the beaten track seems to entice me. I've seen many ranges in my time, but the Flinders continues to enthrall me, its colours changing throughout the day as the sun changes position. The Flinders Ranges is the most underrated tourist destination in South Australia. Tourist authorities spend too much time flogging the wineries of the Barossa Valley and attractions closer to Adelaide rather than the outback and places like the Flinders. Pity, I reckon it is probably the best part of South Australia. As for Arkaroola, it may be pretty expensive for what you get, but with its terrain and geology, even a person with no interest in geology would be blind not to find the country around Arkaroola amazing.

I leave it all behind for now. Another day of travel and we pass over Horrocks Pass and wander through places like Orooroo and on to Peterborough before turning off and heading over the back roads; then we pass places on the Murray such as Murray Bridge and Tailem Bend and over the border back into Victoria. There are countless stories behind me, just from the Flinders to Murray Bridge alone, but I don't have time to relate them here.

I've probably travelled every known road back to Victoria, but the route I'm taking now is one I've done many, many times. I go straight through until I find the turnoff I want.

Southwards – I always get restless when heading south. Home is south of anywhere in the outback. The days continue warm and I am tiring as each day ends. I like to get south and do what I have to do. I rarely spend as much time interviewing when heading for home, usually it is flat out on the outward journey and off I go back home. I look forward to seeing my wife and dog again, feeling the coolness of the mountains near where I live, north of Melbourne, relaxing in the yard, talking to my magpies, and catching up on all the things life at home brings.

'Very much like Seraphine' – Molly gets to hear about her famous auntie.

THE GRAMPIANS TO BALLARAT

JON MUIR AND SERAPHINE SNUPESON, A MAN AND HIS DOG

'Tomorrow will be yesterday and it will be gone.
Make the most of it.'

OK, so you think we are getting close to the end of this trip, and you are ready for home. Not yet. I've arrived at the turnoff and I want to finish by telling you about a man who knows the outback like no other. He is an amazing Australian, someone who can inspire us to do better, to achieve. None of us will ever achieve what he has, but we can all do our bit to lead an interesting life. I've travelled much of his country, but sure as hell not by his mode of transport. So we head off down the Nowhere

Track again, detouring for one last outbacker. His home is in the bush at the back of the Grampian Ranges.

In another era, Jon Muir would be regarded as a world hero and receive adulation wherever he went. But in today's society we applaud sporting heroes more then endurance ones. His achievements – amazing feats of endurance – are what legends are made of. Here are a few of them. He travelled thousands of kilometres by sea kayak, including a 52-day solo journey in 1994. He is the first Australian to have trekked to both the North and South poles (in 2002) and to have climbed Everest alone (in 1988). And he walked across Australia from south to north (in 2001).

Among his peers, in the small club of world-class mountain climbers and adventurers, Jon is regarded as special. To mountaineer Greg Mortimer, 'Jon is in a class of his own.' Adventurer Eric Phillips has this to say about him: 'Jon has done so much ... he's one of the most versatile adventurers on the face of the planet.'

I feel very privileged to have spent time with Jon. He is an ordinary Aussie bloke, down to earth, friendly, matter-of-fact, but he's also incredibly focused, determined, probably demanding, and extraordinary.

I have travelled to his home on acres that back onto the Grampians National Park in western Victoria. Here, too, is his new wife and soul-mate Suzie, a very attractive lady and an amazing woman, who built her home with her own hands and who holds a black belt in karate. Like her husband, Suzie has a love of adventure, but she's also a devoted gardener. She has a quiet, peaceful air about her.

Jon Muir was born in 1961. At age sixteen, after watching a documentary about Mt Everest, he decided to become a professional mountaineer. He climbed extensively in New Zealand and Europe before first visiting the Himalayas in 1982. He has since taken part in five Everest expeditions, pioneering new routes and reaching the summit of Everest alone in 1988.

Jon was awarded the Order of Australia medal in 1989, the Australian Geographic Society's Adventurer of the Year in 2001, and the Centenary Medal in 2003.

Some people have asked him why he didn't get a real job. We discuss how our lives have similar traits. For many years some people didn't see my writing as a real job. But it always was – for me. John laughs as he says, 'I've written a book and made a television documentary in one year. Doesn't that count?' (Yes, it does, mate!)

Anyone who has travelled the outback will know just how amazing his 2001 transcontinental expedition really was. His trek was across some of the toughest and remotest land this country has to offer. John's journey from Port Augusta, on the South Australian coast, to Burketown, on the Gulf of Carpentaria, took in three deserts and two of Australia's largest salt lakes. He crossed only one sealed road and nowhere along the entire route did the population exceed 100. He did all this without a satellite phone or GPS to guide him. All he had was a compass and fifty-five maps; no back-up support. The 128-day trek took its toll, though. By the end of it, he had lost one-third of his total body weight.

Why would anyone undertake such a mammoth task? His reply is simple: 'I want to understand the land in which I live.'

Jon is a hardcore optimist. He likes a challenge, enjoys the natural world, and thrills at trying to understand the land. He says the across-Australia expedition was by far the hardest trek he has done – 'I had this tremendously powerful feeling of being alone.

Not lonely, an incredible sense of being very much *alone*.' He also adds, 'It was the most incredible journey of my life.'

When we first met, I had just returned from a trip across Australia by ute – 14,174 kilometres in twenty days across five states and two territories, much of it on remote dirt roads. I have seen much of the land that Jon traversed; I know how rugged it is. We swapped thoughts about the Sturt Stony Desert. I drove some of it but Jon walked it – he bloody walked it! And a whole lot more. If you haven't seen this part of Australia, you just can't begin to know what Jon Muir achieved. It was a totally bloody awesome effort. Wedged between the sand dunes of the Simpson and Strzelecki deserts, the Sturt Stony Desert is a gibber desert with 'no parallel on the earth's surface', according to its explorer, Charles Sturt, in 1845.

When talking of his life, Jon has a simple philosophy of his incredibly demanding journeys: 'I kinda enjoy the struggle.'

I also want to know more of Jon's sole travelling companion, Seraphine. Having a professional adventurer as your master means you get to see some great countryside. Little Seraphine Snupeson, a Jack Russell–fox terrier cross, led the life of ten dogs, travelling on foot some 2500 kilometres when she set off with Jon on his solo south–north journey across Australia.

'She bonded with me, and wherever I went she went.'

I mention to Jon and Suzie how I've read somewhere that the word 'seraph' is something to do with higher angels. Suzie looks it up in a dictionary as we talk and confirm it, saying that the Hebrew word *seraphim* means ecstatic or fervent. 'She was certainly that,' says Jon. '"Seraphine" is also an old-fashioned French name for angel, and she was definitely angelic as a puppy.'

I ask about Seraphine's other name.

Jon is an expert on bush survival foods.

'Roald Amundsen, the polar explorer, had a dog called Snupeson in the team he took to the South Pole.'

I should have known.

So why did Jon take the little dog on the walk with him?

'Of all the long walks we've done, I'd never done one with a non-human before. I was interested in that. Besides, I didn't want to leave her. She loved to walk. She was my shadow – or maybe I was her shadow, I'm not sure which. I felt we could look after each other.' In the following four months, Seraphine enjoyed something that very few dogs ever experience. She and Jon relied on each other totally for support, comfort, pleasure and mateship. Alone, but totally together.

I have read Jon's book *Alone Across Australia*, but I'm curious to learn more of this amazing little pooch. To walk across Australia from south to north is quite a feat even for a man with a goal and determination. It's a bloody amazing feat for a little dog, who probably wondered, Where the hell are we going? Jon bought Seraphine a special pair of leather, laced booties designed for working dogs, but they were too big for her tiny paws so he had to modify them.

Jon recalls that each day the little dog would have covered twice the distance he did, as she continually ranged all over the place, sniffing here, scratching there, darting off after a bunny, but rarely straying more than 50 metres from Jon the whole time.

Jon had already tried to cross the continent three times before, but had failed each time. Seraphine accompanied him on one of these trips and had also walked the Tirari, Sturt's Stony and Simpson deserts with him.

'The first attempt was the worst. She had a lot of problems with prickles getting stuck in her. Often I put her on the cart and let her ride. Later we made boots with Velcro rather than laces for her feet. After a few weeks she was fine; it takes that long to toughen the feet. She even learnt to remove the prickles herself. Occasionally I still helped her, but about 80 per cent she removed herself.

'A big world for a little dog' – Seraphine digging in the desert.

'We lived off the land, and she'd never dug rabbit warrens until we were out in the desert. She knew and started digging and digging. I gave her a hand now and then but mostly I'd do my own work while she dug. She'd squeal when she got close and I'd put my hand in and take out the rabbit. She got twenty-five rabbits out of ten warrens. And she retrieved about thirty ducks. She also put me onto lizards. She was pretty impressed with herself. Whenever I got the gun out she'd go quiet and get behind me, just by me giving a hand signal. I didn't teach her that – she just knew. She was excited, but knew to be quiet.'

Jon noted in his diary (which he quotes in his book) how 'she is so full of life and enthusiasm for the walk itself that some of it rubs off on me, and given that I am not short of this myself, there is an abundance. Our bond grows stronger by the day and I do worry about my puppy in the wilderness. Dingoes or foxes could kill and eat her, wedge-tailed eagles could carry here away, a snake could bite her – it's a big world for a little dog!'

Seraphine endured whatever her master did each day – rain, heat, lack of food, lack of water. She was totally devoted to the task and to her master. Jon shares his thoughts of the trip with me: 'Water, food, shelter and companionship – they are the most important things in our lives, yet they are all very much taken for granted. They are simply overlooked, unless we don't have them.'

The little dog adapted to her surroundings. 'She felt the cold and always slept in the bottom of my sleeping bag. She also had her own coat. She hated it at first but then she loved it. She would even tell me when she wanted it off, when the morning sun got higher. She had a few coats on the trip, but she had a favourite.'

Jon showed me one coat he'd made from rabbit skin and fur, a tiny bundle held together by Velcro tape. 'In the morning she'd just stay wrapped up and watch me go about getting ready for another day. Sometimes I'd pick up the sleeping bag with her still wrapped up in it and put her on the cart and carry her along until she was ready to walk.'

Then the worst happened. On Saturday, 9 September, 5 kilometres downstream from the ruins of Old Morestone Station, Seraphine Snupeson died. It was day 117 of 'the great mission' and they were just eleven days short of Burketown, their goal. 'It seemed like her death went on forever,' said Jon, but in truth it was all over in about ten minutes. 'I believe she picked up a dingo bait. I had worried about snakebites, but never thought of dingo bait.'

Jon didn't write a lot about her death in his book, just on one page. These few words highlight his pain: 'I held Seraphine in her last minutes and felt her tiny heart beat its last ... surely it can't get any grimmer that that.' Jon tells me he just sat there with her in his arms and cried. It was by far the worst part of the trip. He buried Seraphine and pushed on.

Even sitting at his kitchen bench more than a year later, I see his pain and sense of loss. 'When she died,' he says, 'I almost gave up then. I lost heart. It was the only time I felt lonely. Normally I don't feel lonely. But I felt very lonely. I walked until dark.'

He writes in *Alone Across Australia*: 'Eventually I left with tears streaming down my cheeks into my beard. A large part of me now sees this trip, regardless of the outcome, as a failure. I have failed Seraphine. I failed my own rule of taking good care of my partner/team and I failed in my promise ... to look after Seraphine. It has been a nightmarish day. The only thing to do now is to push even harder. This will distract me from upsetting thoughts, and help me sleep more easily.'

In the following days he felt lost. 'I kept looking for her. I even called out a couple of times.'

Jon looks out the window of the kitchen in silence. I have a lump in my throat. The silence seems total. 'It's so lonely and isolated, but she spent so much time out there I figure that she is now where she belongs.'

Jon did push on and he finally reached Burketown on day 128, 20 September 2001. He had completed over 2500 kilometres – the first totally unsupported traverse of Australia from south to north. He refused food and drink from station owners or any help whatsoever. He even got them to sign declarations to the fact. It had to be his trip. His and Seraphine's. Warren Bonython, desert pioneer of many years' experience, has said of Jon's lone walk across Australia, "I would never have done that."

On the drive home, Jon returned to Seraphine. He found and inscribed a headstone for her grave and said his goodbyes: 'It was difficult to return to the ghostly ruins, though something I felt I needed to do. We placed the headstone on the grave and built a small fence around the lot. Once again I left with tears in my eyes.'

Jon ended up with a new puppy from the same breeder that Seraphine came from, and she is now a part of Jon and Suzie's life.

Molly is a fast and totally active little terror. She growled at me when I arrived, letting me know she was boss. Before long, though, we share plenty of pats and licks. I am amazed at her speed and agility and marvel at her love of life.

'She is very much like Seraphine. She wants to go non-stop and then go some more,' smiles Jon. 'I often tell her about her famous Auntie Seraphine and what a legend she was.'

I ask if Molly will share in adventures with him as well. He thinks long and hard, and it is obvious there's some doubt;

'Alone, but totally together' – Jon Muir and fellow adventurer Seraphine.

memories of losing Seraphine come flooding back. 'I'd like to, but, oh gee, if I lost her too – hmm?' Jon's love of Seraphine was very deep and the bond with Molly is strong. Molly obviously reminds him of the amazing little dog that walked so far and shared so much with him. He doesn't want to loose another mate.

The other dog in the house is Suzies's corgi–fox terrier cross Bagheera. She's boss dog, only no one has told Molly yet. They run and play and go berserk. Molly is the faster of the two.

Jon was completing the television documentary of his trip when I was here. Seraphine is the star. I got to view it prior to its completion for national and international release; and to see that little dog – her interest and keenness, her pride and vitality, her obvious joy and the total faith she placed in Jon – is memorable. She will never be forgotten and has her place in written history. A little dog with a big heart who walked tall beside her master. Jon Muir didn't walk alone across Australia.

He had with him one of the best partners he could ever have gone adventuring with. She will be remembered as Seraphine Snupeson, Queen of the Desert.

I drive away from their home through the tall timbers, filled with satisfaction to have met up with this couple and their dogs, and impressed with Jon Muir's great thirst for life. He has a final word on why we should all step outside our comfort zone and achieve what we want: 'Tomorrow will be yesterday and it will be gone. Make the most of it today.'

The one thing that I believe shows Jon's amazing strength is that by the time he returned home to recover, he had lost a third of his body weight and was in total mental and physical collapse. Yet amazingly, just four months later, he walked to the North Pole.

And he's hardly been idle since then. Dust doesn't get the chance to settle on Jon Muir!

'Some home time' – Jon and Suzie, with Molly and Bagheera.

'In 2004 Suzie and I went off together in sea kayaks for 116 days and paddled from the Daintree River up the east coast of Australia to the very tip of Cape York Peninsula, which was amazing.' Jon had been planning that trip when we first met.

In between major projects, Jon has done numerous short walks. ('You know, just 200 to 300 kilometres, I did a lot of those.')

'In 2006 I attempted a walk to the centre of Australia, which I finally did on second attempt in 2007. I walked from near Port Augusta to 30 kilometres past Mt Zeil in NT, beyond Alice Springs. The spot I walked to is the place furthest from the sea in any direction in Australia. The trip took me seventy days non-stop walking and 1650 kilometres.'

Can you believe this bloke? Like Jon, I read a lot of maps and then drive; Jon reads a map and then walks. He is truly a great Aussie.

So where to from here for Jon and Suzie?

'I'm always plotting some new thing in my life. I'm learning to sail at the moment, still walking, but the best place I go is here – home. I love it, so we're having some home time now.'

By the way, folks, remember I told you about the television documentary Jon was making? Well, it went on to win thirty-four international awards for best documentary, and yes, he filmed his walk of 2007 to beyond Mt Zeil (the highest mountain in the Territory).

Jon didn't take Molly the dog with him, though. 'I couldn't stand the strain of worrying about Molly all the way to NT,' Jon admits.

I look forward to catching up with Jon and Suzie again. They're a great couple, very much in tune with what life is really all about: Memories, achievement, dedication and love.

The towns of western Victoria are behind us and soon we arrive at Ballarat. Sorry, I have to leave you here now; my turnoff is not far along the road. This is where we part company.

When you look at a map of where we've been, you will immediately see that we missed more than we saw. That's the problem with travel – there's always other interesting places just outside the route you've chosen. You can do a circle and just outside the circle is more, so you increase the circle and see more, but then there's more outside the bigger circle, and so it goes on. I've been travelling like this for well over thirty years and the thing that annoys me all the time is that when I look at maps I see all the places I haven't been to.

There is so much I haven't seen, so if this trip has been your first into the outback, let me tell you we have only scratched the surface. Guess we'll just have to go again. Time to have a rest. I'll pick you up again some other time, and we'll share more experiences on the road. You should see where I'm going to take you next time. Wow! Rest up, wash your clothes and pack your bag. You won't know when I'm coming, but I will.

In the meantime, I have a couple of weeks at home and then I head off northeast to Mt Kosciuszko. I'm driving the full length of the Murray River from top to bottom on both sides of the border.

Straight after that you can join me on another outback trip across the Australian landscape. The outback, way out beyond – out where the devil urinates.

I can't wait!

'It's a bitch' – loading the four-wheel drive after the crash.

DON'T LEAVE THE VEHICLE!

Make no mistake, it is a big country. BIG. Real big. Friggin' huge. It is a forbidding place; it has little mercy. Its death grip is as alive today as it always was, before man commenced to 'tame' it. It's a bitch. And you need to be prepared …

It was her very first time behind the wheel of a four-wheel drive. She and her husband had driven just 80 kilometres along the Oodnadatta Track before she rolled the vehicle. It rolled five times. Both were lucky to be alive. Her husband was trapped by the foot, his leg twisted back underneath the seat somehow. It took her half an hour to get out – by smashing the windscreen – and find where the jack was, so she could lift the vehicle up enough off the ground to get some stones under and allow her husband to get free.

My mate Mongrel and I arrived five hours later. We found them in shock: sitting in the sun behind the wreck, with their belongings that they had collected after finding them scattered all over the place. A slab of unopened beer, a cask of white wine, a single 2-litre bottle of water sat in the sun beside them.

As they were in shock, I suggested they move into the shade. *Just one bottle of water!* I couldn't believe it – it kept ticking over and over in my mind. They had hundreds of kilometres to go but just one bottle of (now warm) water between them. The warm wine would have made them sick and the beer would only have dehydrated them.

We stayed with them for a few more hours until the rescue vehicle and trailer arrived. Later we found out that they eventually got home to Adelaide after a two-day bus trip – and were very miserable, sore and stuffed. It could have been much worse. The husband wrote me a letter later to thank us, and commented that he now knew why we stayed with them, and yes they were in shock. Later on, they had a reaction. Now they know why the outback is dangerous. They were lucky. Very lucky.

That happened on one of my trips outback with a mate. They were very nice people. Foolish maybe? No, just inexperienced and unprepared, like many people who travel the outback. Sure, accidents can happen to anyone, anytime, but 'out here' an accident can be a whole heap more dangerous. They were lucky they only had to wait five hours for help to turn up – it could have been five days. And who knows what condition they would have been in by then. Two litres of water between them wouldn't have kept them alive for long.

Being prepared and aware may save your life. I know people with great knowledge of vehicles who think they know it all and could survive anywhere, but most of us know just a little when it comes to outback travel. I'm no expert, but I appreciate the dangers. No matter how careful we are, we can all be caught out.

Never underestimate how dangerous the outback really is. While sand dunes that were barely traversable fifty years ago may now be rough roads, they still claim lives. A few points of rain can turn a rough road into a boggy death trap. You may have to spend at least a week bogged and going nowhere, with no one to come to your aid. It could be blisteringly hot with no water to be found except maybe a dirty puddle, if you are lucky.

And plain old speed can kill too. A German couple touring Australia took their few-months-old baby with them when they went into the desert. The baby became ill and they made a mad rush towards help. Their car rolled and wiped out some trees and all three were killed not too far from Marree. A few white stones in a circle and names scratched in stone, plus a rough wood cross are the only reminder of this family. The accident never made the national news, but it did have an effect on a small community. People down south blamed the condition of the road, but locals knew it wasn't the road, and accident-scene investigations showed high speed to be the cause. I came across the scene and stopped, seeing there had been an accident just recently. I talked to a local resident of the tiny community, who was still upset by the event. He said, 'When are they going to learn?'

People of the outback are faced with this sort of drama often. Ask any local mechanic outback and they can tell you a million stories of what goes on.

One told me, 'They expect the local RAA to come collect them and not pay. When I told a Sydney bloke it would cost $1200 just to collect his car on a trailer, he flipped. What he didn't take into account was the distance I had to go to get it back to the garage, and then ship it south on a truck. And that wasn't by any means an expensive job. We've had many that cost much more than that. I might drive seven hours just to get to a breakdown.'

If you go out into this country unprepared, you may face trouble like you never imagined. Real trouble. Life-threatening.

It's better to have something on board your vehicle – and maybe never use it – than to be stranded in the desert saying, 'I've got one of those, but it's in the garage at home.' I know people who think going with minimal equipment adds to the excitement. They won't think like that when they have a breakdown and don't have any help. If I break down, I'll be staying beside the vehicle until I'm rescued (don't leave the vehicle!), but I will have plenty of water, food and anything else I think I need to survive in relative comfort. Some of the stuff I take with me I have never used – and hope I never do. But I have a satisfied mind, knowing I can survive in the outback for a pretty long time.

Some people think the first and most important thing to pack is the Esky full of beer. The first thing you should pack are the things you really need – the tools for survival – and by that I don't mean mechanical tools. I'm talking of life tools. Make no mistake; your life may depend on it. Water should be the first thing loaded into your vehicle.

Some outback 'specialists' pour scorn on people who carry too much when travelling. I'm of the belief that if you plan carefully and do your research properly you are far better prepared when something does go wrong. That doesn't mean you chuck in everything you can find in the garage and under the sink. Today's vehicles are usually better built and more comfortable and reliable than vehicles in the past, but they're also far more complex. Most people now couldn't work out the complexities of vehicle computers, let alone repair them in the bush like 'in the good old days'.

All you can do now is use what knowledge you have and rely on what parts you have brought with you. Often you simply won't find the parts in the outback, even if you get to some form of civilisation. Chances are that a garage will have to order parts in, which, depending on where you are, could at the very least take some days until they arrive by air or by road.

One other piece of advice: never ignore road signs in the outback – they have been put there for a sound reason. Road conditions can change drastically very quickly. Floods can dramatically change the landscape overnight. What may have been a nice track on your trip out could be a treacherous mud heap by the time you want to come back, and if a sign says the road is closed, then it's closed.

PREPARATION

Maps, first-aid kit, plenty of water, a flint stone, two spare tyres – and two cans of warm beer. These are the first items I pack whenever I go bush. Of course, I take many other things, but these items I never leave behind.

MAPS

Essential to keep you clearly in mind of where you are and where you are going. Don't just rely on GPS or other electronic systems. Often weather may mean you have to detour in the outback, so you need to know exactly where you are and where you are headed. Also, buy a survival book and throw it in the glovebox. Books like these won't take up much room but they all have a wide range of information.

FIRST-AID KIT

You are hundreds of kilometres from help, you are on your own and things happen. It may just be a headache, but it can spoil your trip (out here a headache really can be bad, especially with heat and dehydration). It may be any number of accidents, from cutting a finger to breaking a leg. A good first-aid kit could save your life when no one else can.

WATER

Water is life. Make no mistake in the outback – without it, you can die a terrible death. People have and still do. Don't think there's always water available. There isn't. You can never have enough water with you. If you plan your trip carefully, you should carry many more days of water with you than you think you'll need, just in case of trouble. Yes, they say you can drink your own urine at least once, before it becomes toxic. It has saved people's lives in the outback. Me, I'd prefer a bottle of water. Many outback specialist companies now make water tanks to go onto vehicles. But I'm of the opinion that we shouldn't pack all our water into one container, because if the container leaks it may be empty before you find out. I pack water into numerous containers and bottles – the longer I am going bush, the more I pack. A good, padded cooler pack will hold many bottles.

FLINT STONE

It's cheap and small and you should carry it in your pocket always. If you don't have matches or they get wet or lost or whatever, then a flint will always mean you have fire, and fire gives you warmth and can be used as a distress signal. A flint will always work and give you fire; wet matches won't. And besides, a fire might mean you won't have to eat raw snake. They taste better cooked.

TYRES

If you get a flat tyre, here's a simple way to inflate it. First, you need a couple of things: a length of rubber hose, available from places like Clark Rubber stores, and two hose clamps like the ones that are on the end of a foot pump. You also need to have your spare tyre inflated much higher than normal (check the manufacturer's maximum recommendation). Put a clamp on each end of the hose and hold in place with screw clamps or even plastic zip-ties. If you have a flat, you simply connect one end of the hose to the highly inflated tyre and the other end to the flat tyre. Air will travel from the highly inflated tyre to the flat one – and bingo, two inflated tyres. Simple and easy. I always carry clamps and a hose in my ute.

Totally ripped or blown tyres: sorry, but it won't work and there's no way around it – you will have to change the tyres. The very first thing to do is go sit in the shade and have a cool drink or make a cuppa, then do the job in a more relaxed frame of mind. Being stressed isn't the time to work. Let me tell you, I hate getting blowouts and being bogged – been there and done that in some way-out places, and the adventure wears thin very quickly. I prefer to be prepared.

'Two spare tyres at least' – blowout on the Strzelecki Track.

'Like a knife edge' – tyre change on the transcon railway line.

'Outback tragedy' – The lonely memorial to a German family who lost their lives on the Ooodnadatta Track.

Mind you, it will always happen when you least expect it, and can be very inconvenient. I was to meet a bloke at a certain track leading off the Strzelecki Track one morning when I blew a tyre on my outback caravan, brand-new tyres all round. One blew and I was held up a short time to change it. I never go anywhere without two spare tyres at least. And yes, I have used two spare tyres. On one trip out on the transcontinental railway line (normally off-limits to anyone), between Cook and Ooldea, my mate Mongrel and I had two spares slashed in less than 100 kilometres due to Telstra trucks having gone through before us to service some communication towers, and the heavy equipment meant sandstone rocks on the rough track broke open and ended up being like a knife edge, cutting the walls of the tyres. Remember, often it won't be the tread of the tyre that suffers; more often than not it will be the wall of the tyre.

TWO CANS OF WARM BEER?

Just one of those little tricks you learn from being in the bush. If your car breaks down and catches fire, two warm cans of beer shaken vigorously and then the flip top pulled *partially* back will give you a foam spray like a good fire extinguisher that is capable of putting out a good-sized fire. This saves having to recharge a normal fire extinguisher – and it's much smaller to pack. A car fire could leave you without any water or destroy all your supplies, food, bedding, maps, etc. Then you will slowly die in the open. A car fire could become a wildfire and spread across thousands of hectares and leave you in great danger. (The only thing in your favour is that smoke may attract someone, but don't always rely on it. Out here you may be a long way from help.)

Don't drink the warm beer unless you are in absolute, desperate need, and then don't swallow, just rinse your mouth out. It could dehydrate you more, even if it's cool. It may help you if taken in small doses, but preferably in the cool of night when the desert country can get below zero.

GOING SOLO

Lone outback travel does have its drawbacks. First you have to take extra care and precautions. Sometimes you simply have to think twice about going into areas or doing certain things. I am always checking weather and track conditions.

One of the ways I solved the problem of lone travel, which gives my wife comfort and me extra security, was when I installed a Sat-Trak system in my ute. A great Australian invention, it gives me 24-hour location information anywhere in Australia. They can also be hooked up to mapping systems that on a laptop computer produce large-screen maps. I can drive through Sydney now without dragging out the maps.

The Sat-Trak 24 is not just a GPS to pinpoint your location, but a two-way communication device as well. With a switch of the dial I can send short messages already built in. If I set the dial on 'vehicle', I can send satellite comments such as 'Engine breakdown need help' and then hit the send button. From my ute anywhere in Australia it will send the message to a satellite and then to a communications base in Perth, and the people there can call in the required assistance. If I switch the dial to 'people', I can send messages like 'Heart attack' and they will know exactly where I am and deploy emergency assistance anywhere in Australia. They can also send messages back to me like 'Help on the way'. The system can locate me within 3 feet of anywhere by latitude and longitude. I know where I am because it shows in the small box on the dash.

This system has added a great sense of security to solo travel in the remote areas for me. My only worry is that people not used to outback travel will rely on it too much and think they can disregard all other requirements, believing they can go anywhere without really being prepared.

Don't let anyone tell you that a satellite phone, which is expensive to buy and run, will solve your problems. There are still 'shadows' on the landscape in Australia where sat phones are useless. I often talk with friends and their sat phone always drops out in certain areas.

Remember, it is much easier for an aeroplane to spot a vehicle on the ground than it is to spot a person. Never wander away from the safety of the vehicle – it could mean a long and lonely death. You will always have a better chance of survival by staying with your vehicle, no matter how long you have to wait. Walking in the heat will kill you much faster than waiting for rescue in the shade.

If you do get into trouble, whatever you do, DON'T LEAVE THE VEHICLE!

May your wheel-nuts always be tightened!

Safe travelling.

ACKNOWLEDGEMENTS

As an author who has wandered this great land, I have had the privilege of meeting many great Australians, famous and not, and from all walks of life. This book is the result of the generosity of some people who shared their time with me and told us all of their lives, and also in many cases lent photos as well as allowing me to photograph them in their private domains.

I wish to thank them all for their willingness and for making my role easier. To the outbackers discussed in these pages, my special appreciation – and I raise a glass to you all.

To the other people who assisted in others ways to make my life on the road easier, my thanks. To the dogs of Australia who said g'day, thanks for the memories. To ABC Books, I extend thanks to all those in Sydney who were keen on the project right from the start: publisher Stuart Neal, editor Helen Littleton and copy-editor John Mapps. I look forward to working with you again soon.

Thank you to my long-time literary agent Debbie Golvan, director of Golvan Arts Management, for her continued efforts.

To Janette – who shares the Southern Cross stars of the night sky when I'm a long way from home – and to Dusty the wonder dog, who looks after her when I'm gone. You see me come and go often and I hope you know what drives this four-wheel swagmen in his quest. I do it for you.

Allan M. Nixon 'The Uteman'
Swagman's Rest
November 2007

ABOUT ALLAN M. NIXON

Allan Nixon is a bushie who lives at the base of a mountain range north of Melbourne. Known as 'The Uteman' as a result of his bestselling *Beaut Utes* series of books and *The Bushies*, Allan travels much of Australia writing, photographing and collecting stories for his future works. He has also produced a calendar and a music CD and worked as a consultant on numerous TV documentary film-making projects. His writing and photography have appeared in many magazines and newspapers, including articles and covers for *Outback* magazine. He was an ambassador for Year of the Outback 2006. *The Outbackers* is his nineteenth book, with numerous others in writing or production stages.

'Swagman on his quest' – Allan on the road with a cuppa.

www.ingramcontent.com/pod-product-compliance
Lightning Source LLC
Chambersburg PA
CBHW022038290426
44109CB00014B/899